Mastering Your Fears and Phobias

Mastering Your Fears and Phobias

SECOND EDITION

Workbook

Martin M. Antony • Michelle G. Craske • David H. Barlow

OXFORD

UNIVERSITY PRESS

2006

OXFORD

UNIVERSITY PRESS

Oxford University Press, Inc., publishes works that further
Oxford University's objective of excellence
in research, scholarship, and education.

Oxford   New York
Auckland   Cape Town   Dar es Salaam   Hong Kong   Karachi
Kuala Lumpur   Madrid   Melbourne   Mexico City   Nairobi
New Delhi   Shanghai   Taipei   Toronto

With offices in
Argentina   Austria   Brazil   Chile   Czech Republic   France   Greece
Guatemala   Hungary   Italy   Japan   Poland   Portugal   Singapore
South Korea   Switzerland   Thailand   Turkey   Ukraine   Vietnam

Published by Oxford University Press, Inc.
198 Madison Avenue, New York, New York 10016

www.oup.com

Oxford is a registered trademark of Oxford University Press

ISBN-13 978-0-19-518918-6
ISBN 0-19-518918-3

9 8 7 6 5 4 3 2 1

Printed in the United States of America
on acid-free paper

About Treatments*ThatWork*™

One of the most difficult problems confronting patients with various disorders and diseases is finding the best help available. Everyone is aware of friends or family who have sought treatment from a seemingly reputable practitioner only to find out later from another doctor that the original diagnosis was wrong or the treatments recommended were inappropriate or perhaps even harmful. Most patients, or family members, address this problem by reading everything they can about their symptoms, seeking out information on the Internet, or aggressively "asking around" to tap knowledge from friends and acquaintances. Governments and healthcare policymakers are also aware that people in need don't always get the best treatments—something they refer to as "variability in healthcare practices."

Now healthcare systems around the world are attempting to correct this variability by introducing "evidence-based practice." This simply means that it is in everyone's interest that patients get the most up-to-date and effective care for a particular problem. Healthcare policymakers have also recognized that it is very useful to give consumers of healthcare as much information as possible, so that they can make intelligent decisions in a collaborative effort to improve health and mental health. This series, Treatments*ThatWork*™, is designed to accomplish just that. Only the latest and most effective interventions for particular problems are described, in user-friendly language. To be included in this series, each treatment program must pass the highest standards of evidence available, as determined by a scientific advisory board. Thus, when individuals suffering from these problems, or their family members, seek out an expert clinician who is familiar with these interventions and decide that they are appropriate, they will have confidence that they are receiving the best care available. Of course, only your health care professional can decide on the right mix of treatments for you.

This particular program presents the latest version of a cognitive behavioral exposure–based treatment for specific phobias and severe fears. Specific phobias, which, by definition, prevent a person from leading the life he or she wants to lead and substantially interfere with functioning, represents the most common anxiety disorder, with more than 12% of the population experiencing the distress and suffering associated with this problem. Tens of millions more suffer from severe fears that are also distressing and to some extent disabling but not severe enough to be called phobias. Common examples of these fears include blood injury and injection phobia, in which people experience an actual drop in blood pressure at the sight of blood or injections and may faint. This problem often prevents sufferers from seeking out appropriate medical and dental care. Another common phobia is a fear of transportation, including driving and flying, that prevents tens of millions from visiting relatives, following career paths that require traveling, and so on. Effective treatment can be delivered in as little as one week but is not readily available. Undertaking this program with the help of a skilled clinician offers the best hope yet of relief from the suffering associated with specific phobias and fears.

David H. Barlow, Editor-in-Chief,
Treatments *That Work*™
Boston, Massachusetts

Acknowledgments

The authors thank Julia Blood for her help preparing the original manuscript for revision and suggesting sections to be updated. We are grateful as well to Susan Chang for her assistance in proofreading an earlier version of this workbook. Thanks also to Mariclaire Cloutier, Cristina Wojdylo, and the staff at Oxford University Press for their support and expertise.

Contents

Introduction to Specific Phobias and Their Treatment

Chapter 1

Is This Program Right for You?
The Nature of Specific Phobias

Goals

- ▓ To understand the nature of specific phobias

- ▓ To understand the different types of phobias

- ▓ To determine whether this program is right for you

- ▓ To learn how to use this workbook effectively

The Nature of Specific Phobias

Judy was a career woman in the advertising business who had recently received a promotion. Her new job duties required more traveling than she had ever done before. However, this caused Judy a big problem. Whether it was a half-hour or a five-hour flight, Judy became extremely fearful about the thought of flying, so much so that she had successfully avoided flying for the preceding five years. The last time she flew, she was a "total wreck" for at least a week before the flight. In fact, she was a wreck for the entire time she was away, in anticipation of the return flight. She vowed never to fly again. But how could she give up her job promotion? Judy was terrified that the plane would crash and she would die. She would panic at any unusual sound or movement of the plane. Judy realized that her fear was extreme, but she wasn't able to convince herself to relax. In contrast to her difficulty with travel, Judy was very comfortable with all other means of transportation, including driving on freeways and riding on trains. Judy's life was being impaired by a specific phobia of flying.

Matt had a different type of problem, but it was still a specific phobia. From a relatively early age, Matt became queasy at the sight of blood or injections. He remembers passing out several times, such as when he saw his brother gash his leg and when he was given vaccinations in elementary school. Even bloody scenes on television upset him: he couldn't watch them without feeling weak and lightheaded. At the age of 35, Matt has not been to a dentist for about 12 years because he fears injections. He is afraid he'll faint or won't be able to tolerate the injection. But the pain in his back two teeth is getting worse. Matt is not sure what to do.

Amy is a 55-year-old homemaker and mother of three. She and her husband, Paul, recently moved from New York City to a drier climate and safer environment in Arizona. Amy had not expected the kinds of problems she is currently facing. Within the first few days of moving into their new home, Amy found a lizard on their bedroom windowsill and several lizards in their backyard. She became extremely frightened and felt paralyzed until Paul removed the lizards from her sight. Ever since then, Amy has been living in terror of finding more lizards. She scans each room before entering and dons boots before leaving the house. Amy is suffering from a specific phobia of lizards.

What Are Specific Phobias and Fears?

In a nutshell, a specific phobia refers to an excessive or extreme fear of a particular object (e.g., an animal) or situation (e.g., being in closed-in spaces), along with awareness that the fear is irrational, unnecessary, or excessive (although children do not always have this awareness). Someone whose fear is appropriate given the real dangers of a particular object or situation would not be considered phobic. For example, a fear of being mugged while walking alone in dark alleys in a big city would not be considered a phobia. Similarly, fearing certain deadly insects might not be unrealistic in particular tropical areas, and fears of crossing a deep ravine by means of an old, unsteady bridge would not be viewed as phobic. On the other hand, a fear of falling from a closed office window on the 20th floor of a high-rise building and a fear of harmless reptiles in a zoo are unrealistic—one of the key features of a phobia.

For an exaggerated fear of a particular object or situation to be considered a phobia, the fear must interfere in some way with a person's life or be very distressing. If the fear doesn't bother the person and doesn't interfere with day-to-day activities, then it remains a fear and not a phobia. For example, fears of spiders or snakes may not be considered a phobia for someone who lives in a place where there are no spiders or snakes, simply because the person does not have to encounter the feared object. Also, the person who fears closed-in places, such as elevators, planes, or the backseat of two-door cars, may not be phobic if the fear is relatively mild, is not especially upsetting to the person, and does not impair daily living.

However, the person who is fearful of elevators to the extent that he or she refuses to use elevators, even if it means climbing 15 flights of stairs or moving to a new work location, would likely be suffering from a phobia. Similarly, the person who is so fearful of spiders that he or she refuses to enter the attic or basement or to reach into the back corner of the bedroom closet may be phobic. The person who avoids freeways and drives on side streets for fear of being hit by other high-speed cars is more likely to be considered phobic than the person who feels somewhat uncomfortable in freeway-driving conditions but continues to drive the freeways because it's more convenient.

Being phobic does not necessarily mean that the feared object or situation is completely avoided all the time. For example, a person who is phobic of elevators may continue to use elevators but with a great deal of discomfort or with the aid of certain medications. Similarly, a person who flies several times per year for work may still be considered phobic if each trip is preceded by weeks of worry and sleepless nights about the impending flight. An extreme fear that causes distress and impairment would still be considered phobic, even if the avoidance were minimal. To the degree that your fearfulness of a particular object or situation interferes with doing the things you want to do in your home life, work life, social life, or leisure time, and to the degree that your fearfulness bothers you, the kind of treatment offered in this manual will be helpful.

What Happens When We Are Afraid?

Fear is a very natural emotion. It is a basic survival mechanism that allows us to be physically prepared to escape from real danger (e.g., if a car were racing toward you), or to meet it head on with an aggressive response (e.g., if a person were threatening someone you cared about). That is why fear is often called the fight-or-flight response. The body is activated by a rush of adrenalin whenever we perceive danger (and become frightened), so we can respond quickly by escaping from the situation or finding another way to reduce the potential threat. Many of the sensations we experience when frightened are designed to protect us from potential danger. For example, our hearts race to get blood to the big muscles so we can escape easily. We breathe more heavily to get more oxygen, and we sweat to cool off the body so we can perform more efficiently. The key point here is that fears and phobias are natural emotions that occur whenever a person perceives danger (even when the true danger is minimal, as is the case in phobias).

Fears and phobias are experienced through three separate systems: the *physical system* (which includes a wide range of physical sensations such as dizziness, sweating, palpitations, chest discomfort, breathlessness, feelings of unreality, numbness and tingling, and numerous other feelings), the *behavioral system* (which includes the activities designed to reduce fears and phobias, such as escape, avoidance, and relying on various protective behaviors), and the *mental system* (which includes the fearful thoughts and predictions that contribute to fears and phobias, such as "something bad is going to happen"). The strategies discussed in this book are designed to target these core components of fears and phobias.

Different Types of Phobias

As you may have noticed from the above examples, there are several different types of specific phobias.

One interesting aspect of blood, injury, and injection phobias is that, unlike other specific phobias, the phobic reactions are commonly associated with fainting or near-fainting experiences. Furthermore, more than any other specific phobia, fears of blood, injection, and injury tend to run in families.

Table 1.1 Types of Specific Phobias

Specific Phobia	Feared Objects/Situations
Animal phobia	Dogs, cats, mice, birds, snakes, insects, bugs, spiders, and others
Natural-environment phobia	Heights, darkness, water, storms, and so on
Situational phobias	Driving a car; traveling by train, bus, or plane; closed-in or claustrophobic situations, such as elevators, small windowless rooms, tunnels, crowded places, etc.
Blood-injection-injury phobias	Seeing blood, watching surgery, getting injections, or related situations
Other phobias	All other types of phobias of circumscribed objects or situations (e.g., phobias of vomiting, choking, certain music, novel foods, clowns, balloons, snow, chocolate, clouds)

Note that having one specific phobia does not exclude you from having another specific phobia. In fact, it is not uncommon for people to experience several different phobias at one time. Also, there is some evidence to suggest that having one phobia increases the chances of having another phobia, particularly from within the same general type as the first phobia (such as phobias of spiders and snakes, which are both from the "animal" type).

How Common Are Fears and Specific Phobias?

Specific phobias are the most commonly occurring anxiety disorder. According to a large U.S. survey, approximately 12.5% of the general population reports at least one specific phobia during their lives (Kessler et al., 2005). For many specific phobia types, the proportions differ according to sex, with women reporting more specific phobias than men (Bourdon et al., 1988). It is unclear whether this difference reflects a reporting bias (since it is generally less acceptable in our culture for men to express fear than for women to do so) or a true difference between men and women in the prevalence of phobias. The disparity is smaller for phobias of heights, blood, and needles than for other specific phobia types, particularly animal phobias (Bourdon et al., 1988).

Is This Program Right for You?

The following list of questions will help you decide whether this program is right for you at this time.

1. Are you very fearful of animals, insects, the dark, water, heights, air travel, trains, cars, closed-in places, blood, needles, or another specific object or situation?

2. Do you recognize your fear is excessive, unrealistic, or out of proportion to the true danger?

3. Is your fear interfering with your life or producing a lot of worry and distress overall?

4. Is your fear tied to a phobia of a specific object or situation? Is it a part of another broader problem, such as obsessive-compulsive disorder, panic disorder with agoraphobia, or social anxiety? (If you are

not sure, this question can be answered with the help of your doctor or therapist)

5. Is your specific phobia more disturbing than any other problems or issues you may be experiencing in your life, and therefore deserving of priority attention?

If your answer to all these questions is "yes," then this program is probably right for you.

Alternative Treatments

There are many different treatments that are used to treat specific phobias, including other forms of psychotherapy, hypnosis, and medications, for example. It is important to note that unlike the strategies described in this program, most other approaches have not been systematically studied for the treatment of specific phobias, though it is possible that they may be effective in some cases.

We recommend that if you undertake this program (either on your own, or with the help of a therapist), you should not undergo psychological treatment for your phobias with a different therapist at the same time. As with all treatments focused on the same problem, messages can become mixed and confusing if you are working with two therapists, in two different programs. For that reason, we find it much more effective to do only one treatment program at a time. However, if you are currently involved in another psychotherapy program that is very general in its orientation or is focused on a clearly distinct problem area (such as marital problems), there is no reason that the two cannot be done at the same time. Generally, we recommend that you discuss these issues with your doctor or therapist to decide whether it is best to continue with your alternate treatment, switch to the treatment described in this program, or attempt to engage in both treatments at the same time.

In the case of specific phobias, most experts agree that medications are not a preferred treatment. This is in contrast to other anxiety-based problems, where medications are often useful on their own or in combination with psychological treatment. Note that some individuals may find medication useful to get through a difficult situation (e.g., taking an anti-anxiety medication to cope with a flight); however, there is little research on the use of medications for specific phobias. Rather, there is general agreement that the psychological treatments described in this book are the most effective approach.

Costs Versus Benefits of Treatment

Before going ahead with this program, you must ascertain your level of commitment or motivation to overcoming your phobias at this point. Part of that appraisal depends on knowing what the program entails. You should be prepared an average of five to six weeks of fairly intensive work. The strongest predictor of response to this type of treatment is the amount of practice one is willing to do. The treatment is essentially a learning program that requires quite a lot of work and dedication. The more you put into it, the more you will get out of it. We will be teaching you new ways of thinking and acting, but you must implement these changes. The skills are only as useful as the dedication of the person using them. It is not the severity of your phobia, your age, or how many years you have suffered that determines the success of this program. Rather, your motivation and persistence determine your success. The major costs and benefits are listed below.

Costs

- Time and effort needed to complete the program

- Initial discomfort when confronting specific objects and situations

- Initial increase in stress and fear when confronting phobic objects and situations

Benefits

- Control of your phobia

- Increased quality of life from freedom to comfortably do things you previously avoided

- Higher overall self-esteem from knowing you have conquered a disabling or excessive fear

So, consider whether you have the motivation right now to give it your best shot. If you don't have the motivation right now, or if other things are more important to you, it is better to wait. It is best not to begin a program like this half-heartedly.

How to Use This Workbook

This manual is divided into three parts. The first part describes how specific phobias develop. The second part describes how to treat specific phobias. The third part provides detailed guidelines for overcoming particular types of specific phobias. The first two parts are necessary preliminaries to any chapter in the third part, particularly because many of the terms used are explained in the first two parts. So *read all of the first two parts before proceeding to the chapter in the third part that best fits the kind of phobia you are experiencing*. If you have more than one specific phobia, as people often do, it is probably most effective to begin with the one that is causing the most interference in your daily life or is causing you the most distress and worry overall. For example, let's say you are fearful of dentists and fearful of flying. However, the fear of dentists is currently very problematic because you have a broken front tooth that needs repair, whereas you don't foresee any travel plans for some time. In this case, begin with the fear of dentists. You can deal with the phobia of flying later.

How much time you devote to each part of the manual is mostly up to you. The first part (chapters 1, 2, and 3) consists mostly of explanations, with a few assignments involving assessing and monitoring various aspects of your phobia. It is best to complete the chapters and exercises in this section before moving on to the next section.

The second part (chapters 4, 5, 6, and 7) contains general descriptions of the treatment strategies you will eventually use to overcome your fear, including strategies for challenging fearful thoughts, and strategies for confronting your feared object or situation. The first time you read this part, skim the chapters quickly, just to get a sense of what treatment will involve, but don't do the exercises. You will return to these chapters later.

After you skim the second part, you can turn your attention to the chapter in the third part that is most relevant to your phobia. For example, if you fear cats, you will use chapter 10, which concerns animal phobias. As you work through the chapter in this section that corresponds to your fear, you should return to the chapters in the second part and complete the exercises. The relevant chapter in the third part will give you examples of how to complete the exercises described in the second, so you should read your chapter in the third part before starting the exercises.

On average, the exercises in the second and third parts usually take 5 to 6 weeks to complete for each specific phobia. However, note that it is possible to overcome certain specific phobias (especially phobias of animals, insects, blood, and needles) in even less time. Even a single, prolonged session of exposure-based treatment with a therapist may lead to considerable improvement. Finally, we recommend that this program be done with the supervision of the mental health professional who recommended this manual.

Chapter 2

How Do Specific Phobias Develop?

Goals

- To learn how specific phobias develop

- To learn about prepared fears and belongingness

- To understand the specific ways in which fear develops

- To complete the Fear Acquisition Form

- To learn what factors contribute to maintaining phobias

Why Aren't Feared Situations Random?

When we look at the most commonly feared objects and situations (such as snakes, spiders, heights, and closed-in places) it soon becomes apparent that the things we are most likely to fear are not random. If fear were random, then there would be as many people afraid of flowers as of snakes, and as many people afraid of electrical outlets as of elevators. But there are many more people afraid of snakes than of flowers, and there are many more people afraid of elevators than of electrical outlets. How can this be, particularly given that electrical outlets are more dangerous than elevators?

Well, a psychologist by the name of Martin Seligman has suggested that certain objects are more likely to become feared than other objects because they posed some threat to the survival of the human race over the thousands of years of our existence (Seligman, 1971). Since prehistoric times, objects and situations that threatened the survival of humans have included such things as predators (e.g., poisonous reptiles), heights (e.g., cliffs), the dark (in which a predator might approach undetected), closed-in places (from which it is difficult to escape from a predator or survive without air), and blood (since loss of blood threatens survival). Seligman called these types of fears *prepared*, meaning that humans have a preparedness or predisposition to associate these objects or situations with danger. Because caution in the presence of these objects or situations has been so important to our survival, fear of these situations seems to be "hardwired" in us.

Of course, not everyone is afraid of these situations. The notion of preparedness just means that it is easier for people to *learn* to fear situations that we are "prepared" or hardwired to fear (e.g., certain animals, heights, enclosed places) than it is to learn to fear situations that we are less prepared to fear (e.g., flowers, electrical sockets). For example, let's say that for each of five times that you approached a snake, it hissed at you. Similarly, for each of five times that you walked through a pine forest, hidden branches grazed your skin. Given that a fear of snakes is more "prepared" than a fear of pine trees, it is more likely you would develop a fear of snakes than a fear of pine trees.

Of course, this does not mean that phobias of other objects cannot develop. Clowns, for example, do not represent an object of which we are prepared to be fearful, and yet some people experience a fear of clowns. In fact, over the years we have even worked with individuals flower phobias (a sunflower phobia in one case, and a phobia of hollyhocks in another). However, in terms of overall probabilities, those objects that represent a threat to survival are more likely to become feared than other objects.

Specific Ways in Which Fears Develop

The psychologist Stanley Rachman identified three main ways in which fears develop (Rachman, 1976, 1977). The first way is by *traumatic conditioning*. Traumatic conditioning involves developing a fear after having a direct negative experience with the object or situation. For example, if a person experiences loud barking in the presence of dogs on a number of occasions, he or she might eventually come to expect aggressive barking every time a dog is encountered. In such cases, just seeing a dog would eventually produce fear. Other examples of fears developing from traumatic conditioning include:

- Fear of closed-in places after being trapped inside a closet as a child

- Fear of heights developing after a fall

- Fear of flying developing after a turbulent flight

- Fear of needles after fainting during a blood test

Generally speaking, the more severe the trauma, the more likely that a phobia will develop. Also, if the trauma is strong enough, one experience may be enough to produce the phobic reaction. For example, one experience of being physically attacked by a dog might be sufficient to produce a dog phobia, whereas barking might not lead to a phobia until several barking dogs were encountered. Often, the fear remains for many years after the traumatic event. Think back over your own experiences to see if you can identify a painful or negative event you experienced in association with the object or situation of which you are now afraid.

Traumatic experiences do not explain the origins of all phobias. First, not everyone who has a phobia is able to remember a negative experience causing the phobia to develop (in fact, most people cannot recall such an experience). Also, many people have negative experiences with a particular object and yet do not develop a phobia of that object. For example, not everyone who is bitten by a dog becomes phobic of dogs, and not everyone who experiences strong turbulence in a plane develops a fear of flying. It appears that there are certain characteristics that might predispose some people to be more likely than others to become fearful after a negative experience. These are described in more detail in the section below called "Why me?"

A second way in which specific fears develop is when a person sees someone else hurt in the situation or afraid of the situation. For example, a child who observes his or her mother or father acting afraid of thunder and lightning might develop the same fear. Similarly, seeing someone else hurt in a car accident might cause you to become fearful of driving. This powerful method of fear development is called *vicarious* or *observational.* Much of what we learn is by observation, particularly observation of people who are important to us, such as our parents. Observational learning accounts for much of the reason that fears tend to run in families (more about this later). But remember, just as with traumatic negative experiences, observational learning does not explain everything—many people develop fear without observational learning, and many people have observed others expressing fear of a particular situation without developing fear themselves. Nevertheless, from your own experience, can you identify other people (family members, close friends, or other important people in your life) who were obviously fearful of something that now scares you?

The third reason a phobia might develop is because you were warned or told to be extremely cautious about a specific object or situation. This type of fear development, called *informational transmission* of fears, is also common. For example, parents sometimes instill fears of dogs in children by repeatedly warning their child of the dangers of big dogs. Similarly, hearing news reports about plane crashes can contribute to fears of flying. Again, try to remember whether hearing particularly scary information or receiving lots of warnings from your family or friends preceded your phobia.

Informational transmission can explain how phobias develop when an individual has never had direct personal contact with the feared object or situation. For example, the person who hears about a parent's frightening childhood experiences with snakes may develop a fear of snakes even though he or she lives in a large metropolitan area and has never seen a snake.

So, the three specific pathways through which phobias develop are traumatic conditioning, observational learning, and informational transmission. On the Fear Acquisition form, list experiences or events that seem to represent the three main pathways for the development of your main phobias. A blank copy of this form can be found on page 17. You may photocopy the form from this book, or download multiple copies from the Treatments *ThatWork*™ Web site (http://www.oup.com/us/ttw). An example of a completed form is also available on the Web site.

Remember, these are experiences that occurred *before* you became fearful and that may therefore have caused your phobia to emerge. Also, there might be more than one way in which your fear developed: it is possible that your phobia developed as a result of a personally traumatic experience combined with many warnings from your parents.

Don't be too concerned if you cannot identify traumatic experiences, observational experiences, or informational pathways. Sometimes the original causes for a phobia happened such a long time ago that it is impossible to remember. It is not necessary to your treatment, because the factors that maintain a phobia are not usually the factors that caused the phobia to develop in the first place. The treatment program depends on changing the current factors that contribute to the maintenance of phobias.

Fear Acquisition

Phobia	Traumatic Experiences	Observational Learning	Informational Transmission

Remember that the main pathways of fear acquisition are traumatic experiences, observational learning, and informational transmission, and yet these experiences do not guarantee the development of a phobia. It appears that some persons are more vulnerable than others to becoming fearful. The reasons for individual differences are not absolutely clear, but there are some possible explanations.

The first theory of why some people are more vulnerable to developing fears and phobias has to do with *stress*. Overall, stress (e.g., tension at work, relationship or family conflicts, physical illnesses) tends to lead people to feel the effect of negative experiences more strongly. As a result, people are more likely to feel afraid in situations that would not usually worry them, simply because they are "stressed out." For example, being attacked by a dog might lead to a phobia in someone who is already stressed by family conflict, whereas it might not lead to a phobia in someone whose life has been generally pretty good over the last few months. Also, the person who is overworked and sleep deprived might be much more strongly affected by hearing of a friend who was in a serious car accident than the person whose work pace is regular and unstressed. So, stress can increase the impact of traumatic events, observational learning, or informational transmission, making the development of a phobia more likely.

The second reason that some people are more vulnerable to developing fears and phobias is *biological* and/or possibly *genetic*. As mentioned earlier, there is some evidence that fears run in families, so that the person who is afraid of animals is more likely to have a parent who is afraid of animals (Fyer et al., 1990). Of course, this does not tell us whether the family patterns are due to genetic characteristics or to experiences such as observational learning. In other words, a child may have the same fear as his or her parent partly because of a genetic carry-over and/or partly because he or she observed the parent express fear of the particular object or situation.

Let's assume for the moment that genes do play a role in the transmission of phobias (in fact, several studies suggest this, e.g., Hettema, Neale, & Kendler, 2001; Kendler, Karkowski, & Prescott, 1999). The fact that genes influence the transmission of fear does not mean that the fear is guaranteed to emerge in oneself or one's offspring. Why? Because genetic factors do not account for all fears—at most, they account for only a part of fear development. And the genetic factors involved are not like those of hair color. We do not inherit a full-fledged specific fear of animals, heights, or closed-in situations from our parents, the way we inherit hair or eye color. Instead, genetic factors operate by increasing the chances that the offspring will become fearful—genes lend a predisposition or a tendency that, when combined with other factors, might increase the chances of a particular fear emerging. Genetic predispositions are particularly apparent in the case of blood, injection, or injury phobias (Page & Martin, 1998). It is possible that what is inherited in these phobias is the tendency to faint around blood or needles. The issue of fainting in blood and needle phobias is discussed in more detail in chapter 8.

There are additional biological factors that may seem to cause specific phobias. For example, people with specific phobias sometimes question whether their phobias result from inner-ear problems (particularly individuals who are prone to dizziness upon encountering heights or while driving), poor depth perception or impaired night vision (particularly individuals who are fearful of driving), mitral-valve prolapse (heart murmurs), physical disabilities, hormonal fluctuations, lack of sleep, excess caffeine, and so on. In fact, these types of biological problems may render particular situations more challenging or require the individual to be more careful. However, they do not explain fully why phobias develop in the first place, because there are many people who have the same physical conditions who do not develop phobias. In other words, while some of these biological factors may contribute to the cautiousness with which certain objects or situations must be handled, they are not responsible for the development of excessive fear reactions.

A third factor that may affect the onset of fear is a history of *experience with the feared object*. Let's take the example of a traumatic experience involving a plane's technical difficulties and an emergency landing. Each person aboard the flight will have had his or her own history with flying before that particular traumatic experience. For example, let's say one of the passengers was herself a pilot. Because she had many years experience with flying and probably has a more positive attitude toward flying than most other passengers, she will be less likely to become phobic of flying after the emergency landing. On the other hand, the person for whom this was the very first flight is much more likely to become phobic because he or she has no other positive experiences with flying with which to buffer the negative experience. Similarly, the passenger who loves flying and tries to make a point of traveling every few months will be much less likely to become phobic after the emergency landing than someone who generally dislikes flying and flies only when absolutely necessary. So, people come to a situation with a history of experiences, and previous experiences in the particular situation will strongly influence how people react to a negative trauma. The same of course is true for observational learning and informational transmission. For example, a veterinarian is much less likely to become phobic of horses after observing his or her friend being thrown from a horse than is someone who has had very little experience with animals.

So, the reasons we develop phobias are probably more complicated than you thought. But even this brief description doesn't cover absolutely everything. Elsewhere, the authors have written a more complete and comprehensive account of how biological and psychological factors, including early experiences with the phobic object or situation, interact to cause a phobia to develop (Antony & Barlow, 2002).

Why Do Phobias Persist?

Phobias can persist for years and years, despite full awareness that the fear is excessive or irrational. Why? It is rarely the case that the person continues to be traumatized or exposed to observational learning or informational transmission in ways that serve to continuously re-strengthen a phobic fear. However, any recurrent traumas, negative observations, or warnings from others would certainly contribute to phobia maintenance. There are other factors, called *maintenance factors* that are more responsible for the long-term persistence of fears and phobias.

It is the maintenance factors that this treatment program addresses most directly. Initial causal factors are rarely the same as maintenance factors. In other words, what caused a phobia to develop is usually not what maintains it. There are two principal maintenance factors for phobias—one having to do with avoidance behavior and the other having to do with fearful beliefs.

The first maintenance factor is *avoidance behavior.* If you are afraid of a particular object or situation, it makes sense that you would try to avoid it. Avoidance behavior is a natural coping technique. Avoidance can range from being very obvious to very subtle. For example, you could avoid elevators by using the stairs—this is an example of overt avoidance. Alternatively, you might use elevators but endure the situation by imagining yourself somewhere else—this is an example of subtle avoidance. Similarly, you could avoid spiders by never going into attics or places where spiders tend to hang out (obvious avoidance), or by using chemical sprays in your house much more than is recommended (subtle avoidance). Or you might avoid driving completely (obvious avoidance), or drive only when traffic is slow or on quiet streets (subtle avoidance). Whether avoidance is obvious or subtle, it plays a major role in keeping fear alive. By avoiding, you are in essence confirming the belief that you would be endangered if you allowed yourself to confront whatever it is you fear. In other words, avoidance prevents relearning. Relearning is needed to decrease fear. For example, only by remaining in the presence of a harmless animal will you learn that you are not harmed, and only by remaining on the balcony of a 10th floor building do you learn that you will not fall.

Avoiding discomfort by escaping from a phobic object or situation tends to bring a sense of relief. This relief strengthens the desire to escape: knowing that you feel better when you escape from the feared object or situation means you will be more likely to avoid and escape the next time. Hence, a self-perpetuating cycle of avoidance and fear is established.

Another coping technique related to avoidance behavior is *reliance on safety signals*. A safety signal is anything (for example, a person or object) that makes you feel less fearful, or safer, in the presence of the phobic object or situation. For example, the person who is phobic of driving may feel safer and less fearful when accompanied by his or her spouse. In this case, the spouse becomes a safety signal. Similarly, the person who is phobic of elevators might feel safer and less fearful when there is an emergency phone in the elevator (to call for help if the elevator gets stuck); the phone is a safety signal. Or the person who is phobic of large dogs might feel safer and less fearful when the dog is on a leash: the leash is a safety signal. Experimental research has shown that relying on these and other types of safety signals can be problematic in that the person assumes that survival during a phobic encounter depends on the safety signals, and the phobic object or situation is perceived as being manageable only when safety signals are present. In other words, relying on a safety signal leads one to assume that the phobic object or situation really would be dangerous or threatening if the safety signal were not there; for example, being accompanied by another person in a driving situation is likely to lead the phobic person to fear that he or she would be more likely to have an accident when driving unaccompanied; the safety signal of a phone in the elevator is likely to lead one to fear that he or she would be stuck in an elevator forever if there were no phone, and so on. Therefore, learning to overcome fears involves eliminating both avoidance behaviors and unnecessary safety signals.

The second important maintenance factor has to do with *beliefs,* or what you tell yourself about the phobic object or situation. Phobic beliefs are characterized by a sense of danger, threat, or the view that "something bad will happen." The threat is attached to the particular object or situation, to one's own reactions to the object or situation, or both. For example, a fear of high bridges may persist because of the belief that the construction is generally poor and that the bridge is likely to collapse (i.e., the situation is viewed as threatening), or the belief that becoming fearful on the bridge might lead to losing control of the car and driving off the bridge (i.e., one's own reaction to heights is viewed as threatening). Similarly, fears of animals may persist because of the belief that animals will attack you or that if you become fearful when confronted with an animal it might interfere with your ability to protect yourself or to escape. Finally, the fear of small, enclosed places might persist because of the belief that doors will jam or that if you become fearful in an enclosed place you will suffocate, faint, or lose control. We call these belief patterns *misperceptions* because they exaggerate the actual danger in the situation.

All these beliefs are understandable, particularly if avoidance behaviors have prevented your relearning new beliefs. However, they are damaging because they maintain high anxiety. Why? Because fears and phobias are the emotions that are expressed whenever danger or threat is perceived as likely. So, as long as you perceive yourself to be at risk when you confront your phobic object or situation, fear will continue.

Hence, the main treatment procedures target avoidance behavior and belief systems, with the goal being that you no longer perceive the object or situation as threatening or dangerous. Remember, fears and phobias are feelings that emerge in response to a perceived threat. A phobia, by its very nature, means that your fear is disproportionate to the real threat.

Homework

 ✎ Complete Fear Acquisition form

Chapter 3

Learning About Your Specific Phobia

Goals

- ▨ To identify your phobic objects using the Phobic Objects and Situations form

- ▨ To rate your level of fear using the Bodily Sensations form

- ▨ To identify and record your fearful thoughts on the Thought Record form

- ▨ To identify your coping behaviors on the Avoidance and Coping Strategies form

- ▨ To learn the importance of self-monitoring

- ▨ To spend the next week recording all instances of phobic encounters on the Phobic Encounter Record

Learning About Your Specific Phobia

Self-observation and awareness are crucial to overcoming fears and phobias. Without a detailed record of your own fear and behaviors, it is difficult to choose and implement an effective treatment approach. For that reason, this chapter is devoted to helping you identify all aspects of your phobic reaction. The third part of this workbook will help you refine the procedures outlined in this chapter for specific types of phobias.

What Are Your Phobic Objects or Situations?

As described in chapter 1, there are several different types of specific phobias, and it is very common to have more than one phobia. The Phobic Objects and Situations form provides a fairly extensive list of phobic objects and situations. You may list others at the end if necessary. You may photocopy the form from this book, or download multiple copies from the Treatments *ThatWork* ™ Web site (http://www.oup.com/us/ttw). An example of a completed form is also available on the Web site.

Use a check mark to indicate the situations that you fear and would like to overcome. Now, put the items you have checked in order, ranking them in terms of their priority for treatment. Obviously, items that interfere most with your normal daily routine or cause you most worry and distress overall should be high priorities, whereas items that interfere very little with your life should be ranked lower on the list. Rank the highest priority item number 1, the second-highest number 2, and so on. You may have only one item, or you may have more than one. However, it is probably not necessary to rank more than 10 items.

The top few items will be the phobias that you learn to overcome using the relevant chapters in the third part of this manual.

Fears of Bodily Sensations

Sometimes fear is directed at a combination of the particular object or situation and the physical feelings experienced in response to that object or situation. For example, it is not uncommon for persons who fear elevators to be concerned with the elevator's getting stuck and also with feelings of breathlessness in the elevator. Similarly, a person who is phobic of heights might be fearful of a second-floor balcony but much more fearful of that same balcony if he or she experiences dizziness or wobbly legs when on it. The person who fears flying may be even more fearful if he or she feels hot or short of breath in planes. Driving might be frightening only when one feels sensation of unreality when driving. Fear of needles might become severe only if feelings of faintness occur when around them. As you can see, what is feared can be the object or situation and/or the negative bodily sensations experienced around that object or situation. Why are the bodily sensations feared by some individuals? Briefly, it seems that bodily sensations normally experienced as part of fearful arousal are sometimes misinterpreted as being dangerous. For example, the sensation of shortness of breath might be misperceived as a sign of insufficient air and suffocation in an elevator. Feeling weak in the legs might be misperceived as a sign of increased likelihood of falling over the edge of a balcony.

Phobic Objects and Situations

Instructions: Make a check next to each specific object or situation in which you experience fear. Once you've checked each object or situation that frightens you, put those items in order to indicate how important a priority it is for treatment. Your highest-priority item would be ranked 1, your second-priority item would be ranked 2, and so on. Only rank the items that you checked.

Type	Check	Specific Object or Situation	Rank
Animals and Insects	————	Dogs	————
	————	Cats	————
	————	Mice	————
	————	Birds	————
	————	Snakes	————
	————	Spiders	————
	————	Bugs	————
	————	Other animal (—————————————)	————
Blood, Injection, or Injury	————	Blood	————
	————	Needles	————
	————	Doctors/hospitals	————
	————	Dentists	————
Natural Environment	————	Heights (e.g., balconies, ladders, bridges, ledges)	————
	————	Dark	————
	————	Thunder and lightning	————
	————	Water	————
Situational	————	Closed-in places (e.g., tunnels, elevators, small rooms, stairwells)	————
	————	Driving (e.g., on freeways, city streets, or in poor weather)	————
	————	Airplanes	————
	————	Trains	————
Other	————	Vomiting	————
	————	Choking	————
	————	Other (—————————————)	————
	————	Other (—————————————)	————
	————	Other (—————————————)	————
	————	Other (—————————————)	————
	————	Other (—————————————)	————

The Bodily Sensations form contains a list of commonly experienced bodily sensations. Your task is to identify the extent to which these bodily sensations bother you when you encounter your phobic object or situation. In other words, does your fearfulness of the object or situation increase because of these sensations? Rate each bodily sensation in terms of how frightened you are of the sensation when it occurs around the phobic object or situation, using a scale ranging from 0 to 100. Zero = no fear, 25 = mild fear, 50 = moderate fear, 75 = strong fear, and 100 = as much fear as you can imagine (you can choose any number between 0 and 100).

Your fear of specific bodily sensations might differ from one phobic situation to another. For example, feeling dizzy while driving over a bridge may be frightening when you are the driver but not when you are the passenger, even though being on the bridge is frightening in either case. You can clarify whether your fear of the sensation is affected by variations in the situation in the Comments column. Similarly, your fear of a particular sensation may be high for one phobia but not another. For example, shortness of breath may be very distressing with your fear of elevators but irrelevant with your fear of mice. Therefore, use separate forms to rate your fear of sensations for each of your top three phobic objects or situations. As with the other forms in this workbook, you may photocopy this form from this book, or download multiple copies from the Treatments *That Work* ™ Web site (http://www.oup.com/us/ttw). An example of a completed form is also available on the Web site.

Now, if you rated any of the bodily sensations as being feared at least moderately (at least 50 on the 0-to-100-point scale), then you may benefit from treatment strategies to overcome fear of bodily sensations in addition to strategies for overcoming fear of the phobic object or situation. Both types of strategies are discussed in the second and third parts of this workbook.

Fearful Thoughts

Next, you will identify fearful thoughts. Fearful thoughts in phobias are generally of two types; either they are about being harmed directly by the object or situation or about being harmed by your own feelings or reactions to the feared object or situation. Examples of fearful thoughts of the first type include thoughts of being bitten by a dog, being poisoned by a snake, being trapped in an elevator, being hurt by a needle, being pushed from a

Bodily Sensations

Instructions: For each item, record a number from 0–100 to indicate how frightened you would be to experience the physical sensation in the presence of the situation or object you fear (0 = no fear; 25 = mild fear; 50 = moderate fear; 75 = strong fear; 100 = as much fear as you can imagine. You can select any number from 0–100). Only rate your *fear of the physical feeling* (rather than fear of the object or situation). For example, if you are not at all afraid of sweating when exposed to a snake (regardless of whether the snake itself terrifies you), your fear rating for sweating would be "0." Note that a separate form should be used for each major phobia that you have (e.g., spiders, heights). Record any comments (e.g., "my fear of dizziness is a 75 when I'm driving, but only 40 when I'm a passenger") in the comments column.

Phobic object or situation: _____

Sensation	Fear of Sensation (0–100 scale)	Comments
Racing heart	_____	_____
Shortness of breath	_____	_____
Dizziness, unsteadiness, fainting	_____	_____
Chest tightness	_____	_____
Trembling or shaking	_____	_____
Sweating	_____	_____
Nausea/abdominal distress	_____	_____
Numbness, tingling feelings	_____	_____
Sense of unreality	_____	_____
Difficulty swallowing or choking sensations	_____	_____
Hot flashes or cold chills	_____	_____
Blurred vision	_____	_____
Other (specify _____)	_____	_____

high building, or of crashing in a plane, car, or train. Examples of fearful thoughts of the second type include fears of suffocating from shortness of breath in an elevator, falling from a high place because of dizziness or weakness in the legs, having a heart attack because your heart rate increases when you fly, losing control of the car because you have a sense of unreality when driving, fainting from feelings of weakness during a blood test, and so on.

It is helpful to identify these thoughts because, as outlined in the last chapter, fearful thinking is one of the main reasons that phobias persist over time. It is easier to correct fearful thinking if you can identify what the thoughts are in the first place.

Fearful thoughts can be difficult to identify because they are often habitual, particularly if you have had a fear or phobia for a long time. However, it is generally easier to identify fearful thoughts when actually confronting a phobic object or situation. This can be done by means of a *behavioral assessment*. A behavioral assessment involves approaching the phobic object as closely as you can. At the closest point (or when you decide that you cannot stay in the situation any longer), ask yourself what you are thinking. What thoughts are preventing you from getting any closer, or from staying in the situation for longer? What kinds of things do you imagine happening? Behavioral assessments are easy to do for situations such as elevators or heights, because the feared situations are easy to find. Some behavioral assessments may entail more effort, such as finding a particular animal at a zoo, pet store, or animal hospital. Other behavioral assessments are almost impossible, as for someone who fears flying. However, do the best you can. If you really cannot arrange a behavioral assessment, imagine yourself in the phobic situation and see what thoughts come to mind. For example, the person who is afraid of flying can imagine him or herself in a plane as it takes off, or in the middle of a flight, knowing that there is another hour of flight time to go, and ask "What is it that scares me about the situation—what do I imagine happening in the situation?"

Record your thoughts on the Thought Record after completing a behavioral assessment or imagining the situation. Because thoughts may differ for various phobias, use additional forms to complete thought listings for as many phobic situations as you want. A blank copy of this form is provided on page 29. You may photocopy the form, or download multiple copies from the Treatments *ThatWork* ™ Web site (http://www.oup.com/us/ttw). An example of a completed form is also available on the Web site.

Thought Record

Instructions: Complete a separate copy of this form for each relevant fear or phobia.

Phobic object or situation: _____

Thoughts about the object or situation:

1. _____

2. _____

3. _____

4. _____

5. _____

Thoughts about the way I feel in the situation:

1. _____

2. _____

3. _____

4. _____

5. _____

It might be difficult to identify specific fearful thoughts despite behavioral assessments. That is, you may not be aware of what it is you are thinking . . . you just feel fearful. We will talk more about difficulties identifying thoughts in chapters 4 and 5.

Avoidance and Other Coping Behaviors

Remember from our earlier discussions that avoidance can help maintain a person's fear over time, and avoidance behaviors can be subtle or obvious. Obvious avoidance includes refusing to confront or deal with the phobic object or situation, as well as escaping from it. Subtle avoidance involves strategies for dealing with the object or situation to minimize its impact. The subtle methods of avoidance include distraction, alcohol, medications or other drugs, and overly protective behavior. Examples of overly protective behaviors include dealing with fears of snakes and bugs by wearing excessively heavy clothing and shoes whenever you leave your house, or dealing with a fear of car accidents by driving only in the slow lane of a freeway. Distraction is another means of subtle avoidance. To distract means to take one's mind off the fearful elements in a situation. Like the other methods of avoidance, distraction is a "Band-Aid" method that relieves discomfort in the short term but does not prevent fear from recurring. For example, the person who fears blood and injections may submit to medical interventions only while talking and thinking about something besides the injection. Another example of using distraction is walking across a bridge without ever looking over the rail so as to avoid the perception of height.

Related to the concept of avoidance is reliance on safety signals. As was described in the last chapter, a safety signal is an object or a person with whom you feel safer and less fearful when encountering a phobic object or situation. Common examples of safety signals are spouses, family or friends, portable phones, exit signs, and so on. The particular safety signal is typically based on the content of the fearful thinking. For example, the person who is afraid of losing control while driving would most likely find another person to be a strong safety signal. The person who fears being trapped forever inside an elevator would most likely find a portable phone to be a strong safety signal. The person who is afraid of falling over a balcony might find flat shoes to be a strong safety signal. Safety signals may help you deal with a phobic object or situation in the short term but have the negative long-term effect of leading you to feel as if you cannot manage without the safety signal. Let's take the example of people who believe that the only times they can drive is when accompanied by their spouse. Why is this a safety signal? Because the spouse is viewed as someone who could take over the wheel if the fearful person "lost control." In this case, relying on the spouse prevents the individual from realizing that he or she would not lose control of the car even if unaccompanied.

All these methods of avoidance reinforce misperceptions of danger or threat and provide a sense of relief. Remember, relief reinforces avoidance behavior (as described in chapter 2). In other words, these methods of coping may relieve distress in the short term, but they interfere with overcoming your fear in the long term.

On the Avoidance and Coping Strategies form is a list of types of avoidance. On this form, identify your obvious and subtle avoidant behaviors

Avoidance and Coping Strategies

Instructions: Complete a separate copy of this form for each relevant fear or phobia.

Phobic object or situation: _____

Avoidance or Coping Strategy	Examples

for your main phobia. You may use additional forms to identify patterns of avoidance for other phobias. A behavioral assessment will prove very valuable for on-the-spot observation of what you do and how you cope. In addition, it might be helpful to have a family member, friend, or therapist watch you as you conduct the behavioral assessment. This individual may detect subtle behaviors of which you are not fully aware. A blank copy of this form is provided on page 31. You may photocopy it from this workbook or download additional copies from the Treatments *ThatWork*™ Web site (http://www.oup.com/us/ttw). An example of a completed form can also be found on the Web site.

Now that you have a full profile of the objects you fear, the sensations that increase your discomfort in the situation, your fearful thoughts, and all forms of maladaptive avoidance and coping that contribute to the persistence of your fear, you are in a much better position to make changes. It is necessary to gather this information before proceeding with the rest of this manual.

Over the next week, you may add to the information you recorded today, particularly if you have experiences with your phobic object that provide more information about your thinking and avoidance strategies. In addition, the chapters in the third part of this manual provide more detail for different types of phobias, which will help refine the analysis you have conducted to date.

Self-Monitoring

It is very helpful to keep an ongoing log of your reactions to phobic objects or situations as they occur. Of course, the goal of treatment is to decrease fearfulness and increase approach behavior (i.e., reduce avoidance behavior) to these objects or situations. Ongoing records of your reactions tell us if that goal is being achieved.

It is important to emphasize the value of ongoing monitoring. Years of research have clearly established that our memories tend to become distorted over time. Therefore, when we are asked to recall how we reacted to a particular event, our memory is usually less accurate than on-the-spot recording. Moreover, when it comes to fears and phobias, it seems that our memories tend to distort in the direction of overestimating how fearful we were. That is, you might remember the experience as being worse than it really was. As you can probably imagine, recalling fearful events as being worse than they really were serves only to increase fear of the next encounter with the phobic object. So, monitoring phobic encounters as they occur can actually serve to correct memory distortions and reduce fear of future encounters.

In addition, ongoing record keeping enables you to observe changes over time, in order to see the benefits of your efforts. Otherwise, you might tend to minimize the changes you have made and possibly lose motivation to continue the program. With an objective record of phobic experiences, real changes are more accurately observed.

Finally, ongoing records of encounters with phobic objects and situations help you become an objective observer. Research has shown that control over emotional reactions is increased by taking an objective (i.e., observation-based) perspective rather than a subjective (i.e., feeling-based) perspective. For example, a subjective impression of a phobic encounter would be "I felt terrible, all I wanted to do was get it over and done with, and I never want to do that again." An objective impression of the same situation would be "My fear rating was 60, and I stayed in the elevator for 30 seconds longer than I ever have before." See the difference?

Each time you encounter the phobic object or situation (something you will be asked to do more and more as you begin the treatment phase), complete a Phobic Encounter Record as soon as possible after you have encountered the feared object. If you wait too long, you may forget certain aspects of the situation or your reactions. Begin by recording the date and time of the encounter. Next, briefly describe the situation. For example, a record from an individual suffering from a fear of dogs might be based on unexpectedly coming across an unleashed large dog in the park. Next, rate the maximum level of fear you experienced during the encounter, using the 0–100-point scale (0 = no fear, 50 = moderate fear, and 100 = extreme fear). Then, make a check next to the main bodily sensations you experienced. Also, record any other feelings you may have experienced (e.g., fainting, "rubbery" legs, blurred vision). Next, list thoughts that occurred to you. These thoughts might be negative or positive. Examples of negative thoughts in relation to a dog phobia might be "The dog will jump over the fence and attack me," or "I don't know what to do," or "I will freeze and I won't be able to move until someone comes to help me," or "Its teeth look horrible." Remember to include negative thoughts about the object or situation and about the way you react to the object or situation. Of course,

Phobic Encounter Record

Instructions: Complete a separate copy of this form each time you encounter your feared object or situation.

Date: _____   Time: _____

Situation: _____

_____

_____

Maximum fear (use a 0–100 point scale): _____

Main bodily sensations (check)

Racing heart _____	Shortness of breath _____	Dizziness/unsteadiness _____
Chest tightness _____	Nausea _____	Sweating _____
Trembling _____	Numbness _____	Choking _____
Hot/cold _____	Sense of unreality _____	

Other feelings: _____

_____

_____

_____

Thoughts: _____

_____

_____

_____

Behavior: _____

_____

_____

_____

as you proceed through your treatment program, these negative thoughts will be replaced by adaptive, coping-oriented thoughts. Finally, record how you reacted (in other words, your behavior). Did you stand still, move away quickly, call for help, take medications, close your eyes and hope it would go away, hold on to something or someone for protection, and so on? Remember to include obvious or subtle avoidances, such as using distraction, overprotective behavior, or medications, or relying on safety signals. Again, by the end of the treatment program, these negative avoidant behaviors will be replaced by coping and approach behaviors. A blank copy of the Phobic Encounter Record is provided on page 34. You may photocopy it from this workbook or download multiple copies from the Treatments *ThatWork*™ Web site (http://www.oup.com/us/ttw). An example of a completed form is also available on the Web site.

The Phobic Encounter Records provide valuable information to discuss with your mental health professional, who may be able to help you work on changing specific thoughts and behaviors. If you are dealing with more than one phobia, we recommend that you tackle one phobia at a time, starting with the phobia that is currently causing the most trouble. Use the Phobic Encounter Record in reference to the particular phobia you are tackling at a given time.

Homework

✎ Complete Phobic Objects and Situations form

✎ Complete Bodily Sensations form

✎ Complete Thought Record

✎ Complete Avoidance and Coping Strategies form

✎ Over the next week, complete a Phobic Encounter Record each time you are exposed to your feared object or situation.

General Principles of Treatment
for Specific Phobias

Chapter 4

Developing a Treatment Plan

Goals

- [ ] To learn about in-vivo exposure and other treatment strategies
- [ ] To determine which treatment strategy is most appropriate for you

Developing a Treatment Plan

As we mentioned in chapter 1, there are different types of phobias (animal, natural-environment, situational, blood, injection or injury, etc.) that warrant slightly different treatment approaches. So, use the information you summarized about your own phobic reactions in chapter 3 (typical physical sensations, behaviors and thoughts) and information you may have recorded over the last week on Phobic Encounter Records when considering the options provided in this chapter.

Exposure to the Phobic Object or Situation

We know from years of research that the method called *in-vivo exposure therapy* is particularly effective for overcoming specific phobias. In fact, many experts agree that exposure is a necessary component of treatment for specific phobias. In brief (exposure methods are described in detail in chapter 7), in-vivo exposure involves repeated, systematic, and controlled encounters with the feared object or situation in order to learn that your fears are unfounded (of course, this is only appropriate for "irrational" fears, as is the case for specific phobias). You have probably heard the old adage that the best thing to do after falling off a horse is to get back on again and continue riding. Well, in-vivo exposure follows the same basic premise.

The method of in-vivo exposure has been investigated in many studies at our centers and other centers around the world. In fact, exposure has been found to be effective for treating fears of spiders (Antony, McCabe, Leeuw,

Sano, & Swinson, 2001; Hellström & Öst, 1995; Muris, Mayer, & Merckelbach, 1998; Mystkowski, Craske, & Echiverri, 2002; Mystkowski, Echiverri, Craske, & Labus, in press; Öst, Ferebee, & Furmark, 1997; Öst, Salkovskis, & Hellström, 1991; Rowe & Craske, 1998; Tsao & Craske, 2001), snakes (Craske, Mohlman, Yi, Glover, & Valeri, 1995; Gauthier & Marshall, 1977; Hepner & Cauthen, 1975), rats (Foa, Blau, Prout, & Latimer, 1977), thunder and lightning (Öst, 1978), water (Menzies & Clarke, 1993), heights (Baker, Cohen, & Saunders, 1973; Bourque & Ladouceur, 1980; Lang & Craske, 2000), flying (Beckham, Vrana, May, Gustafson, & Smith, 1990; Howard, Murphy, & Clarke, 1983; Öst, Brandberg, & Alm, 1997), enclosed places (Öst, Johansson, & Jerremalm, 1982; Craske et al., 1995), choking (Greenberg, Stern, & Weilburg, 1988), dental treatment (Gitin, Herbert, & Schmidt, 1996; Moore & Brødsgaard, 1994), blood (Öst, Fellenius, & Sterner, 1991), and balloons (Houlihan, Schwartz, Miltenberger, & Heuton, 1993).

For some phobias (e.g., phobias of animals, injections, dental treatment), a single session of in-vivo exposure lasting two to three hours can lead to significant improvement in up to 90% of individuals (Antony, McCabe, Leeuw, Sano, & Swinson, 2001; Gitin et al., 1996; Öst, 1989; Öst, Brandberg, & Alm, 1997; Öst, Salkovskis, & Hellström, 1991), usually with long-lasting results (Öst, 1996). For other phobias (e.g., driving phobias, claustrophobia), more sessions may be needed, but significant improvement is still very likely following exposure. Also, the likelihood of maintaining your improvements over time increases when you continue occasional practices after formal treatment is over.

So, the chances of success with these types of programs are very high. As mentioned in chapter 1, success depends on practice and effort on your part. But obviously, the benefits are major and the chances are definitely in your favor. Let's maximize your chances by combining the basic method of exposure with the most appropriate additional strategies that address your thinking patterns and fears of bodily sensations.

Changing Your Thoughts

As we described in chapter 2, negative thoughts and misinterpretations of the danger of an object or situation play a very important role in keeping a phobia alive. For example, anyone who believes that he or she is helpless in the face of particular animal and that he or she could be seriously injured by that animal is likely to be fearful. Why? Because fears and phobias are generated by the perception of threat. The question that has to be asked is whether the perception of threat is realistic. Obviously, phobia treatment is based on the premise that the perception of threat is unrealistic.

Now, beliefs about the object or situation seem to vary from one person to another, not only in the content of the thought but in the ease with which negative thoughts can be identified. That is, some people are able to identify many negative thoughts, whereas others report that they are not aware of negative thoughts so much as the feeling of fear. Let's take fears of elevators as an example. Some persons are able to clearly identify thoughts such as "I will be stuck in here forever," or "I will go crazy if the elevator gets stuck," or "The elevator cables will break." Others have less-conscious negative thoughts and may be more likely to report "I just feel terribly afraid and I don't know what of. I know the elevator is unlikely to get stuck and that I would probably make it even if it did get stuck, but still I am afraid." Of course, negative thoughts are likely to be operating in both people, but one person is more able to describe his or her thoughts or has more-specific thoughts than the other person. Strategies that focus on changing negative thoughts by discussing and questioning them may be more valuable for the first person than for the second person. Nevertheless, we recommend that everyone read chapter 5 in the second part entitled "Changing Your Thoughts."

The methods described in chapter 5 are called *cognitive therapy* techniques and involve using careful questioning and logical analysis to modify fearful thought patterns. Such techniques have been found to be very helpful for many different anxiety disorders and may also be useful for specific phobias in which clear misinterpretations exist.

In summary, if you are easily able to identify negative interpretations about the phobic object or your reactions to it, chapter 5 will be particularly helpful. However, even if it is difficult to identify negative thoughts, we recommend that you still read chapter 5.

Fear of Sensations in the Phobic Situation

In chapter 3, we discussed the role of fear of your own reactions in phobic situations. That is, what is frightening to some people is not only the particular object or situation but also the physical sensations that are experienced. For example, the person who is afraid of heights may fear the rail or the edge of the escalator in addition to fearing the feelings of weak legs or dizziness that are experienced when up high. Similarly, the person who is fearful of driving may be fearful of fast cars on highways and of experiencing a racing heart or a sense of unreality while driving on highways.

When fear is directed at both the phobic object and one's fearful physical reactions, treatment should target both aspects. Methods for dealing with fear of sensations are described in the second part of chapter 7. Just as with a fear of objects or situations, the fear of sensations that occur in phobic situations is overcome by systematic exposure to those sensations and by changing fearful beliefs concerning the sensations.

There are three clues for assessing whether you should practice exposure to physical sensations. First, if you checked several physical sensations on the Bodily Sensations form, then fear of physical sensations likely plays an important role in your response to the phobic object. The second clue is if you were readily able to identify fearful thoughts about the physical feelings you experience in phobic situations on the Thought Record. Examples would be fears that shortness of breath means suffocation, weakness in your legs means you could fall, or "raciness" inside means you are about to lose control. Finally, exposure to physical sensations will be particularly important if thoughts on your Phobic Encounter Records refer to fears of losing control, going crazy, dying, or endangering yourself as a result of the way that you physically feel in the phobic situation.

Regardless, we recommend that you read the sections of chapter 7 concerning exposure to physical sensations; however, if your fear of physical sensations is minimal, there is no need to practice exposure to sensations. Your exposures can instead focus on the situation or object you fear (also discussed in chapter 7).

Summary of Treatment Methods

While your treatment will definitely involve repeated exposure to the phobic object or situation, it may or may not be done in combination with (1) special emphasis on changing thoughts and/or (2) reduction of fear of sensations that occur in the phobic situation. The second part of this manual provides details of each therapeutic strategy. The third part of this manual describes how to incorporate each type of strategy (exposure to feared situations, changing thoughts, and exposure to feared sensations) for specific types of phobias.

Homework

✎ In the coming week, continue self-monitoring using the Phobic Encounter Record each time you encounter your phobic object or situation.

✎ Review this chapter and determine which treatment strategies are most appropriate for you.

Chapter 5

Changing Your Thoughts

Goals

- ◼ To learn to change your negative thoughts

- ◼ To learn about the types of distortions in phobic thinking

- ◼ To use the Changing Phobic Thinking form prior to each phobic exposure practice

Changing Your Thoughts

Negative thoughts play a major role in maintaining fears because the perception of threat, even when no threat really exists, naturally generates fear. Therefore, learning to correct misperceptions of threat is very helpful for overcoming excessive fears. As mentioned before, not everyone can readily identify negative thoughts in phobic situations. Nevertheless, misperceptions and fears of dangerous things happening are central to fear and avoidance behavior. Think about it, if you truly believed that the elevator would *not* get stuck, or that you would *not* be trapped, or that you would *not* suffocate, then your fear of elevators would most likely be drastically minimized. Or if you truly believed that the rail would not collapse, that the balcony was sturdy, and that you would not fall over the edge, then your fear of heights would most likely disappear. Likewise, if you truly believed that the snake was harmless and you knew exactly how to handle it, then it probably would not be a feared object.

Sometimes, negative thoughts result from a lack of information or from inaccurate information. Therefore, the first step toward changing thoughts is to gather accurate information, either from experts, books, or other reliable sources. The second step involves more directly examining distortions in thinking that occur when you are very anxious, and learning ways to challenge such distortions. Both steps are outlined in this chapter.

Fears are often based on a lack of information or on inaccurate perceptions. Let's look at some examples. Fears of snakes and spiders are sometimes based on the assumption that snakes and spiders are inevitably poisonous or aggressive. In fact, most spiders and snakes are not poisonous and, when handled in the right way, are unlikely to attack. Also, fears of elevators are frequently based on the assumption that getting stuck could lead to suffocation or that the elevator cables could snap at any moment. In fact, there is always ventilation in elevators, and it is almost unheard of for elevator cables to break (the mechanical features of elevators are checked regularly). Fears of flying are often related to misperceptions about the vibrations, movements, and sounds heard during flight. In fact, most of these vibrations and sounds reflect the normal operation of a plane, and others reflect aspects of flight that are not at all indicative of an impending crash. Fears of injections are sometimes based on the misperception that the needle will cause great pain and injury, whereas the pain is often mild, and the damage caused by the insertion is minimal.

It is important to gather realistic information to fill gaps in knowledge and to correct blatant misperceptions with respect to the particular object or situation you fear. There are two basic approaches to educating yourself about your phobic object or situation. The first is to read anything and everything you can and to talk to experts as much as you can to obtain a complete overview. The second strategy is to list your major concerns (which you did to some extent in chapter 3 in the Thought Record) and to find information relevant to each concern. The second approach is more efficient than the first approach because it focuses your information search on facts that are relevant to your particular fearful thoughts.

How can you find the information you need? To start, the Internet is a great source of information (but beware—it is also a great source of misinformation!). Also, several airlines offer courses for those afraid to fly that provide extensive information about all aspects of flying (there are also several great books on this topic). Veterinarians and pet stores will have lots of information and books about animals. Elevator companies can provide information about the operation and safety features of elevators. Be selective in your information sources; choose the true experts, because some unreliable or biased sources may only add to your misinformation. Examples of biased sources may include sensationalistic news shows, certain Web sites, friends who share your phobia, and people who have experienced a trauma in the situation.

Becoming Educated About Your Reactions to the Feared Object

Sometimes, the physical sensations that occur as a result of becoming fearful are misinterpreted as reflecting impending loss of control (e.g., "the sense of weakness is my arms means I can no longer control the wheel of the car and I will drive over the side of the road"), an inability to cope with the current situation (e.g., "I am frozen and I can't move when I am on a balcony"), or enhanced danger (e.g., "this shortness of breath means there is not enough air in this elevator and I am going to die of suffocation"). Since these types of interpretations of the physical sensations are very frightening, it is understandable that fear and panic result. In fact, fear of the sensations is likely to increase the strength of the phobic reaction. Therefore, the original fear of the phobic object or situation is magnified by an additional fear of the physical sensations that occur while you are exposed to that object or situation. In addition, fear and panic produce more physical sensations, and therefore a cycle of sensations, fear, sensations, fear, and so on, is produced as well. Fear of physical sensations tends to be more strongly associated with situational phobias (such as driving, flying, and enclosed places) and blood and injection phobias (especially a fear of fainting) than with animal phobias. Although the sensations may be frightening, they are not dangerous. They are not associated with loss of control, heart attacks, suffocation, collapsing, paralysis, or most of the other outcomes that people sometimes fear. As discussed earlier, they are part of a normal fear response.

Changing Phobic Thinking

Errors in thinking occur during states of fear and anxiety because one is especially alert for threat or danger. Consequently, it must be appreciated that phobic thoughts tend to be biased in the direction of over-perceiving danger, even when no real danger exists. Hence, an important step toward changing underlying fearful beliefs in phobic situations is to treat thoughts as hypotheses or guesses rather than as facts. Once you recognize them as hypotheses and not facts, they are open to questioning and challenging. Given that phobic thoughts tend to be distorted anyway, questioning and challenging is particularly important; the goal is to develop alternative, more realistic ways of thinking. There are two main types of errors that occur in phobic thinking—*overestimation* and *catastrophic thinking*. We will consider each of these in turn.

Overestimation

Overestimation is essentially the same as jumping to negative conclusions. It involves treating negative events as being probable when in fact they are unlikely. Examples include:

- Assuming that a dog will probably attack, even though most people are never attacked by a dog; even among people who have been attacked, the vast majority of encounters with dogs are not associated with aggression

- Predicting that a plane will crash, even though the odds of a flight crashing are close to zero

- Predicting that the car will crash, even though the odds of crashing during any particular car ride are very small

It is useful to examine why negative overestimations persist despite evidence to the contrary. Of course, one reason might be that you have consistently avoided your phobic object or situation, so that you have not gathered evidence to the contrary. Another reason that negative overestimations persist has to do with the tendency to attribute your survival in the presence of the phobic object or situation to your reliance on safety signals and other overprotective behaviors (e.g., "I only made it because I managed to keep away from the edge," "If my wife hadn't been there to hold on to me, I could have lost control and fallen over," "If I had looked over the edge then I might have fallen," or "I would have fallen if I had stayed there any longer") or to "luck," instead of realizing the inaccuracy of the original prediction. In reality, you did not fall because the real chances of falling are almost zero, regardless of how close you are to the edge, whether you are alone or accompanied, whether you look over the rail or not, and regardless of how long you stay on the balcony.

A third reason that misperceptions persist is because people tend to pay close attention to information that confirms their beliefs, and they tend to ignore information that is inconsistent with their expectations. For example, an individual who fears thunderstorms will be particularly attentive to articles in the newspaper about people who have been struck by lightning. However, some statistics estimate that the chances of dying from a lightning strike are about 1 in 2 million. As frightening as some tragic news stories might be, they rarely provide accurate information about the probabilities of danger.

To counter the biased tendency to seek out information that may not be accurate, it is important to actively search for information to contradict your beliefs. This may not come naturally and it may take some effort. For example, instead of focusing on the 1 person in 2 million who dies from a lightning strike, pay attention to the other nearly 2 million individuals who don't die this way. Only by actively seeking out alternative information can you come close to arriving at the truth.

Catastrophic Thinking

The second type of error arises from viewing an event as "dangerous," "unbearable," or "catastrophic," when, in actuality, it is not. This error is called *catastrophizing* or *catastrophic thinking*. Examples of catastrophic thoughts include:

- "I can't cope with the fear anymore. I just can't deal with freeways."

- "Snakes are gross. I can't stand to look at them."

- "The pain of an injection is unbearable. It's the worst thing I can imagine."

- "Feeling fearful in an enclosed place would be awful."

All these examples frame the object of fear in a context that is horrific and replace an objective coping method with a sense of unmanageable fear. Decatastrophizing involves realizing that the occurrences are not as "catastrophic" as previously stated and is achieved by considering ways in which negative events might be managed instead of thinking about how "bad" they are. For example, instead of focusing on not being able to cope with fear while freeway driving, one focuses on what can be done to overcome the fear, such as driving short distances at a time. In other words, decatastrophizing entails learning to focus on behavioral accomplishments as opposed to negative feelings. The person who focuses on the pain of injections might replace such negative thoughts with realizations that the pain is short lived and that other perhaps more intense pains have been survived in the past. Or the person who is fearful of animals could consider ways of approaching, touching, and handling an animal effectively instead of worrying about the inability to cope or move. When you come right down to it, most phobic situations are manageable to some degree. No matter how intense your fear is, you will survive. Decatastrophizing involves looking at things in perspective and realizing what can be achieved as opposed to automatically assuming that the situation is unmanageable.

Summary of Strategies for Challenging Phobic Thinking Distortions

In summary, there are two main errors that characterize phobic thinking. These are overestimating the likelihood of negative events, and catastrophizing the meaning of phobic encounters. While these types of errors are natural, given that the whole purpose of anxiety is to alert us to the possibility of danger, they contribute to the persistence of unnecessary fear. The steps toward correcting thought distortions are as follows:

1. Identify negative thoughts in the phobic situation.

2. Treat negative thoughts as guesses instead of facts and realize that other interpretations exist.

3. Classify negative thinking as either overestimations or catastrophizing.

4. For overestimations, question the evidence, obtain more accurate information, and identify more realistic alternatives.

5. For catastrophizing, recognize means of coping instead of dwelling on your perceived inability to cope.

Using the Changing Phobic Thinking Form

The Changing Phobic Thinking form provides a structure for identifying and challenging negative phobic thinking distortions. This form requires listing the event, or how the phobic object was encountered, documenting your original fearful thinking patterns, questioning the probabilities of negative overestimations, and developing alternative probable outcomes and cop-

Changing Phobic Thinking

Instructions: Each time you experience anxiety or fear in relation to your phobic object or situation, complete this form. In the first column, record the event or situation that triggered your fear. In the second column record your initial fearful predictions and thoughts. In column 3, record realistic alternative thoughts about the situation. In the last column, record the extent to which you believe your initial thought was true, after considering all the evidence (use a 0–100-point scale, where 0 = definitely not true, and 100 = definitely true).

Event	Initial negative thoughts	Alternative outcomes and coping orientation	Realistic probability of initial negative thought coming true (0–100)

ing orientations. The alternative probable outcomes and coping methods refer to (1) what is a more likely outcome than the fearful outcome you first imagined, and (2) what is a realistic way of coping with the situation. The realistic probability Column is rated on a 0–100-point scale, where 0 = no chance at all of ever happening, and 100 = definitely will happen. The probability rating is realistic because it considers all the evidence. As with the other forms in this workbook, you may photocopy the form from this book or download copies from the Treatments *ThatWork*™ Web site (http://www.oup.com/us/ttw). An example of a completed form is also available on the Web site.

It is recommended that you use this form prior to each phobic exposure practice, as described in the third part of this manual. In the meantime, however, you can practice in relation to phobic encounters that you recorded over the last week or so using the Phobic Encounter Record. That is, transfer phobia encounters onto the Changing Phobic Thinking form by listing the phobic situation and negative thoughts you previously identified and adding alternative outcomes and realistic probabilities.

Planning for the Next Steps

Before beginning to use the strategies discussed in this chapter, we recommend that you first read chapters 6 and 7 in this workbook, followed by the chapter in the third part of this workbook that corresponds to your fear. For example, if you are fearful of flying, you will read chapter 13. When you read the relevant chapter, you will be directed to return to the strategies discussed in this chapter, and you will be shown how to integrate these strategies into your treatment.

Chapter 6

Getting Ready for Exposure

Goals

- To prepare for exposure

- To learn how exposure helps reduce fear

- To develop an exposure hierarchy

Preparation

The next step is to understand and prepare for exposure. Remember that exposure refers to repeatedly and systematically confronting the object of your fear. One of your first responses to the idea of exposure therapy might be "I can't do that, that's the reason I'm seeking help; otherwise, I would have done it on my own a long time ago." Or you might feel that it is too painful to go through a program of having to confront the very thing you have been trying to avoid. The truth, however, is that it is very difficult to overcome a fear without confronting the feared object. This is true even if you have never before come face to face with the object of your fear. Changing your thoughts in the ways described in the previous chapter may help reduce your fear, but in the majority of cases, thoughts are more effectively changed as a result of repeated and controlled direct practice with feared objects or situations.

Another possibility is that you may have tried exposure in the past only to find that it did not work. Reasons that exposure may not have worked in the past include the following:

1. You may believe you have done in-vivo exposure when in fact you have not. For example, being forced into a situation is not the same as setting up a specific target to practice repeatedly. A one-time drive on the freeway is not the same as driving on the freeway three to four times a week in order to overcome a driving phobia. So, it is impor-

tant not to confuse difficult or negative one-time experiences with true in-vivo exposure therapy.

2. Attempts at repeated practices may not have been done frequently enough. For example, walking down an enclosed stairwell once a month is much less effective than stairwell practice several times per week to overcome a claustrophobic reaction. There is the related possibility that any single practice was not continued for long enough. Spending 90 minutes a day practicing approaching a snake will be much more effective than practicing just 5 minutes a day. There is more about this in the next chapter.

3. Distracting yourself while practicing in your feared situation may detract from the benefits of exposure. So, your attempts at exposure may have been thwarted if, for example, you practiced walking out onto a balcony while trying to keep your mind occupied with other images. Similarly, all forms of subtle and obvious avoidance that you identified in chapter 3 will work against the benefits of exposure. For example, looking for an exit sign when walking through an underground parking garage will detract from the benefits of exposure practice for the person who is claustrophobic. Relying on the presence of safety figures, like friends or family, may help you confront phobic situations initially but will detract from the benefits of exposure in the long run unless you eventually make a point of practicing exposure without your safety figures. Walking up to a rocky area in your backyard where lizards are frequently found will be less effective if you persist in wearing large boots and gloves to protect yourself.

So, if your previous attempts at exposure have been unsuccessful, consider whether any of these factors may account for the lack of success.

Why Confront Objects That You Have Tried to Avoid?

As discussed in earlier chapters, avoidance interferes with learning to overcome your fear. Avoiding a feared object prevents learning about ways of coping with a situation and prevents learning that what you are most worried about rarely, if ever, happens. For example, how can you be completely convinced that you will not fall off a balcony if you don't ever walk out onto a balcony? How can you ever fully realize that you will not die from suffocation in an elevator, even if it were to get stuck between floors, unless you practice riding in elevators? Avoidance interferes with learning even when it is a subtle type of avoidance. Let's take the example of refusing to look at an injection while blood is being drawn. If you do not look at the injection, fearful thoughts such as "the needle will damage the skin badly" or "the needle will be very large" remain intact. Only by looking at the injection can an individual learn that the skin is not damaged badly and/or the needle is not as large as was expected.

Exposure Hierarchies

Exposure therapy begins with developing a very specific list of situations that represent progressively more-difficult encounters with your phobic object or situation. As described in the next chapter, this list of situations will guide your exposure practices.

Usually, the list of situations is generated from particular themes relevant to how much fear is experienced. For some people, the theme might be proximity to the object—for example, five feet away from the balcony edge is easier than two feet away. For others, the most important theme is time, such as staying in small room for 10 minutes as opposed to 20 or 30 minutes. Another theme is size: a large animal is scarier than a small animal. Additional themes to consider are presented in the chapters from the third part of this workbook. A sample hierarchy for a fear of heights is provided below. Additional sample hierarchies (for other common phobias) may be found on the Treatments *ThatWork* ™ Web site (http://www.oup.com/us/ttw).

Sample Exposure Hierarchy for Fear of Heights

1. Standing on a chair

2. Standing on a table

3. Standing 10 steps up on a ladder

4. Looking out of a 12th-floor closed window

5. Looking over a second-floor open balcony

6. Looking over a fifth-floor open balcony

7. <u>Looking over a tenth-floor open balcony with water below</u>

8. <u>Looking over a tenth-floor open balcony with concrete below</u>

9. <u>Crossing the 9th Street bridge</u>

10. <u>Ski lifts</u>

The first step in developing your own hierarchy is to choose the theme or themes important to how much fear you experience in relation to your main phobia (the phobia you have chosen to begin with). Next, generate a list of about 10 items that incorporate different levels of these themes. The list is to include a range of situations, some that are easy and some that are quite difficult. So, for example, the person who is afraid of driving may include driving long and short distances, on busy and quiet roads. The person who is afraid of flying might include short and long flights, in small and large planes. The person who is afraid of spiders might include little and big spiders, in a glass tank and on a tabletop. The items in the hierarchy should be quite specific and detailed. For example, "looking at a spider in a glass jar from three feet away" is a much more useful item than "looking at a spider."

Now, in the spaces provided on the Exposure Hierarchy, generate a list of about 10 situations that reflect an array of easier and more difficult situations with respect to your main phobia (there is space for up to 12 items). Don't worry about making this list of situations perfect, because you will have a chance to revise and/or refine your list when you get to the third part of this manual. List the situations in order of difficulty, with the most difficult items at the top and the easiest items on the bottom. Now, in the Anxiety column, rate each situation on a 0–100-point scale to represent what your level of anxiety would be if you had to face that situation right now. On the 0–100-point scale, 0 = no fear, 25 = some fear, 50 = moderate fear, 75 = strong fear, and 100 = extreme fear. You can choose any number from 0 to 100.

This is your exposure hierarchy. You may choose to start your exposure at the lowest ranked item or you can start higher up the list (as described in the next chapter). You may photocopy this form from this book or download multiple copies from the Treatments *ThatWork*™ Web site (http://www.oup .com/us/ttw). An example of a completed hierarchy form is also available on the Web site.

Exposure Hierarchy

Instructions: In the first column list about 10 situations related to your phobic object or situation, ranging in difficulty from extremely difficult to only mildly difficult. In the second column, rate the extent to which each of these situations would trigger anxiety or fear (0 = no anxiety or fear, 100 = maximum anxiety or fear). List the items in order of difficulty, with the most difficult items listed near the top, and the least difficult items listed near the bottom.

Situations	Anxiety (0–100)

Because of your fear, it may be very difficult to follow through with many of the tasks necessary for the successful treatment of your phobia. For example, it may seem almost impossible to get the items that you need (e.g., spiders, photos showing blood and injury) for exposure practices, and it may be difficult for you to stay in your feared situation (e.g., standing at a high place, being on an airplane, or driving on the highway) without someone with you, especially at the beginning of treatment. Therefore, one of the first things you should do is find a helper. If possible, it is best to have a trained therapist coach you during exposure sessions. However, if this is not possible, your helper can be a friend, relative, or spouse—as long as they are not frightened by the types of situations that you fear.

You and your helper should come up with ways to create the situations on your hierarchy. The chapters in the third part discuss places where you can obtain items that you might need. Your helper can assist you in obtaining these items if you are unable to do so on your own. Your helper will also be able to demonstrate the different practices for you before you do them. For example, having your helper practice finger-prick blood testing on him or herself will help you learn that these tests are not painful or dangerous. Observing your helper perform activities that frighten you will help decrease your fear.

In addition, the helper should be supportive, willing to answer questions and provide information about the situation, praise you when you make progress, provide humor, and show empathy during exposure sessions. If you typically faint, scream, shake, or cry during exposure to the feared situation, your helper should be prepared for it. Many people incorrectly view crying and screaming as signs to stop conducting the exposure or to take a break. You and your helper need to know that it is normal to cry, scream, and shake during practices. These are not signs to stop but rather signs to continue the exposure until you have learned that your feared consequences don't occur or that you can cope with what happens.

Your helper must understand that he or she is to be responsive to your needs. You will be the one who determines what you are willing to do during practices. The helper's role is to help you achieve your goals. On the other hand, the helper should be firm and not give up too easily. You should consider your helper's suggestions carefully before deciding whether to move to the next step. We recommend that your helper read the relevant sections of this workbook.

Planning for the Next Steps

Before beginning to use the strategies discussed in this chapter, we recommend that you continue to read the next chapter (chapter 7) in this workbook, followed by the chapter in the third part of this workbook that corresponds to your fear. For example, if you fear heights, you will read chapter 11. When you read the relevant chapter, you will be directed to return to the strategies discussed in this chapter, and you will be shown how to integrate these strategies into your treatment.

Chapter 7   *How to Do Exposure*

Goals

- ▦ To learn how to do exposure exercises
- ▦ To use the Exposure Rating form
- ▦ To learn the difference between massed exposure and spaced exposure
- ▦ To learn the difference between graduated exposure and intense exposure
- ▦ To learn the difference between controlled escape and endurance
- ▦ To compare imaginal exposure and in-vivo exposure
- ▦ To learn to deal with fear of physical sensations
- ▦ To learn ways of maintaining your progress
- ▦ To learn ways of dealing with the most common obstacles that arise

How to Do Exposure

By now, you have examined your responses; identified the objects, situations, and physical sensations that you fear; and recorded the anxiety-producing thoughts and avoidance behaviors that contribute to your phobia. You have also begun to identify and challenge specific distortions in your thinking about the phobic object or situation, such as overestimations and catastrophizing. You have learned why exposure therapy works and have developed your own hierarchy of situations. Before beginning to practice exposure, there are a few guidelines that should be taken into account:

Duration and Number of Practices

Exposure is most effective when practices *last* long enough for you to learn that whatever you were most worried about happening never or rarely happens or for you to learn that you can cope with whatever it is you are facing. For example, if you are afraid of heights and you believe you can stand on a balcony for 10 minutes without collapsing and falling over, but you are worried that you might indeed collapse and fall over the balcony if you were to stand there for 30 minutes, then clearly it will be important for you to practice for the 30 minutes, so that you can truly learn that what you are most worried about does not occur.

Similarly, exposure is most effective when you repeat the practices enough *times* for you to learn that whatever you are most worried about happening never or rarely happens, or for you to learn to cope with whatever it is you are facing. For example, if you are afraid of driving and you believe you could drive one exit on the freeway one time without losing control of the car, but you are worried that you would indeed lose control of the car if you repeated that one exit drive more than three times, then clearly it will be important for you to practice that exit more than three times.

By staying in the situation, despite your fear, you will learn that whatever you are most worried about never or rarely happens or that you can cope with whatever was causing you to feel fearful. Eventually, your fears and phobias will decline, but it is not important for your fears and phobias to decrease in the moment that you are facing your phobic situation—through lengthy and repeated practice, the fears and phobias will eventually decline.

So, plan for practices that will last at least 30 minutes, and preferably an hour or more, so that you can practice facing the phobic situation for the length of time or the number of times that you believe will most effectively help you realize that what you are most worried about is unlikely or that you can cope. Do not base the duration of the practice on how much fear or anxiety you experience but rather on what you decide up front is the most effective length or number of repetitions.

If your fear becomes overwhelming during a particular practice, it is fine to take a break. However, get back into the situation as quickly as possible after leaving. Remember that avoidance can reinforce your fear over the long term.

Spacing of Exposure Practices

Exposure works best when practices are spaced close together. For example, it is better to practice every day (often called *massed exposure*) than to practice once or twice per week (often called *spaced exposure*). We recommend that you practice at least three or four times per week, particularly at the start of your treatment. Practicing more frequently is even better, though it is a good idea to take a day off at least once per week to give yourself a rest and help consolidate your learning. As treatment progresses and your fear decreases, it is useful to space your practices to consolidate what you have learned.

Graduated Versus Intensive Exposure

Exposure can be done in a graduated format, progressing at a comfortable pace from the least to the most difficult items. This progressive approach is called *graduated exposure*. The alternative approach is to begin exposure with a more difficult item or to move through the items on the hierarchy more quickly. This is called *intensive exposure*. Each approach has its advantages, but your fear will eventually decrease either way. With intensive exposure, you will get over your phobia sooner, although you will be likely to experience more intense discomfort along the way. In addition, by tackling the more frightening situations earlier, the remaining less frightening items on your hierarchy will become easier. With gradual exposure, it will take longer to get over your phobia, but the process will be less intense. Also, by progressing gradually, the more difficult items on your hierarchy will become easier as a result of building confidence with the earlier, less difficult items.

In general, the recommendation is to go as fast as you are willing to go. It helps to push yourself a bit, but you don't have to go to extremes unless you want to. If you find that you have taken a step that is too big or too frightening, it's OK to slow down and add smaller steps before moving on. However, intensive exposure may be appropriate if you are facing a fast-approaching deadline by which time you want your phobia to be significantly reduced (for example, an upcoming flight, in the case of a flying phobia).

How far should one go in exposure practices? From our experience, it seems that going beyond what one would normally do is very helpful, particularly in terms of long-term maintenance. The more you do, the less likely that your fear will return later on. So, include final steps at the top of your hierarchy that are particularly challenging (though not dangerous). Examples might include having a spider crawling on your arm (if you are afraid of spiders), staying in enclosed places for prolonged periods of time (if you are claustrophobic), or going to the top of the tallest building you can find (if you are afraid of heights).

Behaviors During Exposure

There are several ways you can complete an exposure practice. One way is to race through it, hoping that you will make it all the way and desperately wanting it to end as soon as possible; another is to proceed with excessive caution and hesitation. Yet another way is to do all aspects of the task as though you were not fearful. For example, let's say your exposure task was to walk across a bridge. You could accomplish this task by walking very quickly across the bridge without ever looking over the edge (notice the subtle avoidance strategies). Alternatively, you could walk at an average pace, stopping every so often to look over the rail. In the long run, the second approach is most likely to help you overcome your fear.

The first approach may be the only way you can accomplish the task the first few times. That is, you may succeed only by walking briskly while looking straight ahead as you cross the bridge. However, the practices should continue until you can walk slowly and look over the edge of the bridge. In other words, all the obvious and subtle avoidance behaviors that you identified in chapter 3 should eventually be eliminated so that the task can be accomplished without any avoidance strategies at all. Remember, these include distraction, overly protective behaviors, medications, and safety signals. Eventually, though not necessarily at the beginning of your practices, each item on the hierarchy should be practiced without the aid of your usual subtle avoidance strategies and safety behaviors.

Predictability and Knowing What to Expect

From years of research, we have discovered that predictability lessens fears and phobias. In other words, knowing what to expect generally makes a task easier. That's why it usually helps if patients are told before surgery what kinds of medical procedures they will undergo and what kinds of physical discomforts to expect after surgeries. The same principle applies to exposure practices. Although you cannot know everything that might happen, it will help to have some accurate expectations about both the phobic object or situation and your reactions to the situation.

In terms of expectations about the phobic object or situation, the information that you gather will help (as described in chapter 5). From reading or talking to various "experts," you will learn more about the characteristics of snakes, planes, or whatever it is you fear. In addition, plan ahead in terms of each specific exposure practice. For example, let's say the task is driving on a freeway. Before your first practice, it might be helpful to go as a passenger with another driver on the same road, just so you will have a chance to learn more about the features of the road (e.g., how the road curves). Or, before you receive a blood test (an item on your hierarchy of blood and injection fears), ask the nurse how long the procedure will take and what to expect during the test. Before you attempt to touch a dog, ask the owner how the dog usually reacts to being touched. The fewer the surprises during the initial exposure practices, the better. Of course, as you become more confident, the surprises won't matter so much.

Imaginal Versus In-Vivo Exposure

A phobic object or situation can be practiced in real life (in other words, in-vivo exposure) or in one's imagination. We recommend in-vivo exposure, since the effects tend to be better. However, imaginal exposure is particularly valuable under certain conditions, such as when it is impractical to conduct repeated exposures to the feared object or situation (e.g., in the case of flying or storm phobias). Imaginal exposure is also useful when your level of fear is so intense that you are unwilling to begin with direct confrontation. If so, imaginal exposure can be an early item on your exposure hierarchy. In other words, you may begin by imagining the phobic situation enough times that it can be imagined without undue fears, then progress to real-life practice with the phobic situation.

However, there are some disadvantages to imaginal exposure as well. For example, imagining is not always easy, and not everyone can imagine well. If it is very difficult for you to picture the phobic object or to experience fears as you imagine the phobic object, then imaginal exposure may not be helpful. Also, imaginal exposure does not necessarily lead to less fear when the phobic object or situation is finally confronted in real life. In other words, imaginal fear reduction does not lead to actual fear reduction in all cases. For these reasons, imaginal exposure should be followed by real-life exposure, if at all possible.

Completing the Exposure Rating Form

After each time a specific item on your hierarchy is practiced, rate the maximum level of anxiety you experienced on the Exposure Rating form. This form allows you to record several pieces of information. First, list the date of the exposure practice and the item from your exposure hierarchy that is being practiced. Next, indicate which practice this is—the first time for this particular item, or the second, third, fourth, and so on. Finally, rate the maximum level of anxiety you experienced by using a 0–100-point scale, where 0 = no anxiety, 25 = mild anxiety, 50 = moderate anxiety, 75 = strong anxiety, and 100 = extreme anxiety. You may select any number between 0 and 100. Feel free to photocopy the Exposure Rating Form from this book or download multiple copies from the TreatmentsThat *Work* ™ Web site (http://www.oup.com/us/ttw). An example of a completed form is also available on the Web site.

Overcoming Fear of Bodily Sensations

In chapter 3, you rated the degree to which you were fearful of sensations such as a racing heart, shortness of breath, trembling, sweating, difficulty swallowing, and so on that might occur when you encounter your phobic object or situation. Fears of these bodily sensations are usually based on misperceptions that the sensations are dangerous. For example, feeling a sense of weakness in your legs when standing on a 10th-story balcony may be misperceived as indicating you are likely to fall over the balcony. Similarly, feeling short of breath while standing in an elevator may be misperceived as indicating insufficient airflow and suffocation.

As you can see, misperceptions of the sensations can only intensify the fear you already experience in response to the phobic object or situation. It appears that people who are afraid of the physical sensations they experience in their feared situations may benefit from exposure practices that specifically target the fear of sensations felt when confronting the feared object or situation. Once your initial fear of the object or situation has decreased, you can step up the intensity of the exposure by adding exercises designed to bring on the sensations you fear. However, if you are not bothered by the physical sensations experienced in the phobic situation, then you may skip this section.

Otherwise, begin by thinking up ways of deliberately bringing on the sensations that bother you. These should be methods that you can apply when you are facing your phobic situation. Again, the idea is to learn that not only is the object or situation not dangerous but it is even safe to be in the situation while experiencing intense physical sensations. For example, the woman who is afraid of feeling weakness in her arms while driving could

Exposure Rating

Instructions: This form should be used each time you complete an exposure practice. In column 1, record the date. In column 2, describe the exposure practice (e.g., what did you do?). In column 3, record the practice number (e.g., if this was the second time you practiced that item, you would write "2"). In the last column, record the maximum level of anxiety or fear you experienced, using a scale from 0–100 (0 = no fear; 100 = maximum fear).

Date	Exposure description	Practice number	Maximum anxiety (0–100)

induce a sensation in her arms by tensing them for 30 seconds at a time and feeling the weakness afterward. The person who is afraid of feeling short of breath in an elevator could overbreathe (that is, take fast and very deep breaths) to induce shortness of breath (of course, this would not be appropriate if there are strangers in the elevator). The person who is afraid of feeling off balance when at heights could shake his or her head from side to side a few times when standing on a balcony. Below is a list of exercises that can be used to induce feared physical sensations while confronting phobic objects or situations:

1. Drive with the heater on and windows rolled up (heat)

2. Wear wool clothes, jackets, or turtlenecks (heat) when using elevators

3. Turn your head quickly (dizziness, off balance) when on a high balcony

4. Hold your breath (shortness of breath) when in an elevator or other enclosed place

5. Take a few fast and deep breaths (breathlessness, tingling, lightheaded) when in an elevator or other enclosed place

6. Drink a cup of coffee (agitation or racing heart) when in any phobic situation

As mentioned earlier, you can practice exposure to the phobic situation first without the deliberate induction of physical sensations and then practice exposure to the phobic situation at the same time that you deliberately bring on the physical sensations that bother you.

Be sure to minimize any forms of subtle avoidance. In the case of sensations, subtle avoidance may take the form of doing an exercise lightly so as to avoid intense sensations, or limiting your practices of the exercises to when someone else is around in the event that you need help (this would be OK at first, but eventually you should be able to induce the sensations on you own).

How to Deal With Your Thoughts in Exposure Practices

It may not matter how much exposure practice you do if your thoughts do not change. As was mentioned earlier, fearful thoughts tend to change naturally as a result of repeated practice, but sometimes they may become stuck, and it helps to challenge fearful thoughts directly. As was described in chapter 5, fearful thoughts are challenged by obtaining accurate information, and by identifying and challenging specific distortions in thinking. So, it is important to spend some time examining your expectations and thoughts about the upcoming task before every exposure practice.

Before each exposure practice, list all your negative thoughts about the specific task. What is it you are most worried about happening? As you do this, go beyond the thought of becoming fearful and identify which worries lead you to become fearful, or what worries you about becoming fearful in the situation. Next, consider whether the thoughts represent overestimations or catastrophizing: to what extent are you overjudging the likelihood of negative things happening during your exposure, and to what extent are you viewing the situation as being much more unmanageable than it really is? (Review chapter 5 if you are unsure of these terms.) Next, challenge those thoughts by examining the evidence and recognizing alternative, more realistic ways of thinking. By rehearsing new ways of thinking before the exposure task, you will be better able to use the more realistic interpretations when confronting the feared object. Use the Changing Phobic Thinking form shown in chapter 5 to help you question your thoughts before each exposure task.

Changing your negative phobic thinking patterns is important during and after exposure practices as well. As fear builds during the exposure practice, ask yourself key questions:

■ What is it that I think could happen?

■ How likely is it that it would happen?

■ What is realistically more likely to happen?

■ What will I do to cope with this situation?

After the exposure practice is completed, it is very important to go back over the experience in your mind. Evaluate what happened and what you might do differently next time. Watch out for unhealthy self-criticism. Remember, if you felt fearful during the practice, that is OK—in fact, it is expected. You will learn more effectively if you experience some fear. Also, remember what you have done as opposed to how you felt. For example, it is much more helpful to reward yourself for having driven two miles on the freeway rather than criticize yourself for feeling fearful while you were driving. Similarly, reward your accomplishments; for example, reward yourself for touching a feared animal instead of criticizing yourself for not handling the animal more than you did.

Every accomplishment, no matter how small, will contribute to your progress. It is almost always the case that behaviors change sooner than feelings. In other words, you will be able to confront the object sooner than you will feel comfortable doing so. With continued practice, levels of fear will decrease.

Maintaining Treatment Gains

Once you have overcome your fear, the next step is to ensure that it never returns. The best way to do this is to continue occasional exposure whenever you have the chance. It will be important to never avoid or escape from the feared situation in the future. For example, if you have overcome a fear of dentists, be sure to keep regular appointments. If you once had a fear of spiders, make an effort to get as close as possible to harmless spiders when the opportunity arrives to ensure that the fear doesn't return. If you have overcome a fear of driving, be sure to drive occasionally after the fear has decreased. The more you practice exposures in different situations, the better. You may find that you get used to receiving needles from one particular doctor but still have difficulty with unfamiliar doctors. Doing your practices in a variety of situations and contexts will help ensure that this does not happen.

For most people, the success that they experience following treatment will be long lasting. However, occasionally individuals experience a return of their fear. This can happen for at least two reasons. First, you may encounter a situation that is much more difficult than those that you had practiced earlier. For example, although you may have successfully gotten over a fear of driving over the bridges in your neighborhood, you might still find the prospect of driving over larger bridges (e.g., the Golden Gate Bridge in San Francisco) very frightening. If you discover a new situation that triggers fear, approach the new situation as just another practice. Similarly, you may encounter your previous phobic object or situation in a completely new context, such as would happen if you had successfully overcome your fear of spiders in rooms but then came across a spider as you were walking through your backyard. Read this chapter again and use the strategies discussed in the chapter to cope with the new situation or context.

A second reason that an individual's fear might return is that the person went a long time without encountering the feared situation. If this happens, it may be necessary to reread the material in this chapter and to begin using some of the strategies a second time. Fortunately, it is usually easier to get over the fear the second time than it was the first time.

A third reason your fear might return is that you are enduring a life stress (e.g., marital conflict, stress at work or school, financial problems). During stress, people usually experience a chronic state of increased arousal (e.g., increased breathing, heart rate). Therefore, a slightly fear-provoking situation that might normally be manageable might be enough to push someone "over the edge" and lead to a strong fearful response. Usually, when the stress subsides, your fear will return to the pre-stress levels. However, it may still be important to increase the frequency of your exposure practices during or immediately following a stressful time, particularly if you start to get the urge to avoid the situation again.

Finally, fear sometimes returns in individuals who later experience a traumatic event in the feared situation. For example, a painful surgical procedure may trigger a return of a medical phobia, being bitten by a dog may cause a return of a dog phobia, and getting into a minor car accident may cause a driving phobia to return. If a negative experience triggers a return of your fear, it is very important *not* to start avoiding again. Rather, you should make every attempt to get back into the feared situation and practice until your fear eventually decreases, according to the principles described in this manual.

Troubleshooting

Here are some challenges that may arise during the course of exposure therapy, along with suggested solutions.

Problem: My fear is not decreasing during my exposure practice.

Solution: This is OK. The goal is not to immediately decrease your fear, and in fact it is beneficial to remain fearful because that gives you invaluable experience—the experience that you can tolerate fear and anxiety. Maintain the goal of doing practices that are sufficiently long and repeated a sufficient number of times for you to learn that whatever you are most worried about never or rarely happens and that you can cope with what you are facing, even when fearful. Eventually, your fears and phobias will decrease.

Problem: Even though my fear decreased during my practice, I was fearful again the next time I tried to practice.

Solution: This is normal. That is why we recommend repeated exposure. Between sessions, some fear will return. It should be less each time (on average) and eventually it will no longer be a problem.

Problem: It is hard for me to think straight during exposures.

Solution: You may find that in the situation you fear, it is difficult to use the cognitive coping strategies discussed in chapter 5. With practice, these strategies will become second nature and easier to use. Also, even if you don't use them perfectly, just doing the exposure practices will help decrease your fears and phobias by disproving your fearful predictions.

Problem: I'm not sure if I have the willpower to do this.

Solution: The treatment strategies described in this manual are very difficult. You may feel like you don't have the motivation to carry out the practices that we recommend. There are several ways to deal with this. One way is to generate a list of all the reasons that you want to overcome this fear. List all the things you will be able to do. Think about the future payoff and not the short-term discomfort. Reward yourself for completed sessions. Make a list of potential rewards (going out for dinner, watching your favorite TV show, taking a day trip, etc.). Decide in advance how you can reward yourself after each session. But don't give yourself the reward unless you do what you plan.

Summary

Exposure can be done in a number of different ways. Here are the most important guidelines to ensure that exposure therapy is effective:

1. *Practices should be prolonged and repeated so that you can learn that whatever you are most worried about rarely or never happens and that you can cope.* Conduct exposure practices of 60 minutes or longer.

2. *Practices should be frequent and spaced close together.* Practice at least three or four times a week, with at least one day off per week. Later on, spread out your practices to consolidate what you are learning.

3. *Progress as quickly as you are willing to go.* In other words, choose either a graduated approach, by starting with the least fear-provoking item and progress up to the most fear-provoking item on your hierarchy, or use a more intensive approach by starting with more fear-provoking items.

4. *Know what to expect during practices.* Before each exposure practice, develop realistic expectations of what is likely to happen and how you are likely to react. Practices should be as predictable (i.e., have as few surprises) as possible, especially in the initial stages of treatment.

5. *Identify and challenge fearful thoughts.* Before each exposure practice, identify negative fearful thoughts, challenge overestimations and catastrophizing, and develop more realistic alternative ways of thinking.

6. *Focus on your behavior rather than your feelings.* After each exposure practice, evaluate what you accomplished as opposed to how fearful you felt. In fact, expect to feel fearful during exposure practices.

7. *Don't fight fearful feelings during practices.* If you feel intense discomfort during practices, do not fight the feelings. Rather, allow yourself to feel fearful. Fighting the feelings will only increase your discomfort.

8. *Do not use subtle forms of avoidance during practices.* Practice each item on your hierarchy until you can do the task without subtle avoidance, such as distraction, overly protective behaviors, medications, and safety signals.

9. *Go beyond what you would normally want to do.* After completing all the items on your hierarchy, go a step further and practice a situation

that you might not normally encounter (e.g., practice having a spider crawl on your arm, or look over the highest balcony you can find).

Planning for the Next Steps

Before beginning to use the strategies discussed in this chapter, we recommend that you read the chapter in the third part of this workbook that corresponds to your fear. For example, if you are fearful of driving, you will read chapter 12. When you read the relevant chapter, you will be directed to return to the strategies discussed in this chapter, and you will be shown how to integrate these strategies into your treatment.

Strategies and Ideas for Various Specific Phobias

Chapter 8

Phobias of Blood, Needles, Doctors, and Dentists

Is This Chapter Right For You?

This chapter is for you if you answer *yes* to the following:

1. Do I have an unrealistic or excessive fear of needles, the sight of blood, or visiting the doctor or dentist?

2. Does the fear cause me distress or interfere with my life? For example, Does it bother me that I have this fear? Do I avoid places or activities because of the fear? Is my lifestyle affected by the fear?

3. Am I motivated to get over my fear?

4. Am I willing to tolerate temporary increases in fear and anxiety or discomfort to get over my fear?

What Is a Blood or Needle Phobia?

A blood or needle phobia is an excessive or unrealistic fear of being in situations that involve blood, injury, or injections. A blood or needle phobia typically leads to avoidance of the situation and, by definition, must cause significant distress or impairment in a person's life. For example, if a person fears needles but has no reason to come in contact with them, his or her fear would not be called a phobia. On the other hand, a medical student who is afraid of seeing blood might be diagnosed with a phobia because it could interfere with his or her training as a physician. Similarly, avoiding dentists despite tooth pain could be a sign of a dental phobia.

People with blood and needle phobias tend to avoid a variety of situations in which most individuals feel comfortable. Some situations that are avoided include watching television programs or movies showing violence or medical procedures, visiting hospitals, giving blood, and going to the doctor or dentist. In addition, individuals with blood phobias are less likely to pursue medical careers such as nursing and dentistry or to take classes that involve dissection (e.g., high school biology).

Like people who fear blood, individuals with needle phobias often avoid doctors and dentists. In addition, they may delay immunization shots and medical tests that involve needles (e.g., blood tests). Individuals with needle phobias may prefer to undergo medical procedures (e.g., dental work, childbirth) without anesthesia to avoid receiving an injection. They may even avoid making life changes that require blood tests (e.g., applying to college, getting married, or beginning a new job).

In addition to a fear of blood or needles, other common reasons for avoiding doctors and dentists include fear and anxiety over finding out that one has a serious illness (e.g., cancer), fear of pain (e.g., from a dentist's drill), fear of embarrassment or of being judged negatively by the doctor or dentist (e.g., being embarrassed to undress in front of the doctor, being embarrassed about poor dental hygiene), and fear of having one's blood pressure or pulse measured.

Like other phobias, blood and needle phobias are associated with extreme fear. However, people with this type of phobia also tend to experience disgust when exposed to blood, surgery, injury, or other related situations (or images depicting these situations). In fact, for some people, disgust is even stronger than fear. Fortunately, the strategies described in this workbook (especially the exposure-based ones) usually help decrease levels of both disgust and fear. Treatment seems to work well, regardless of whether the primary emotion is disgust, fear, or a combination of the two.

Blood and Needle Phobias and Fainting

Unlike most other phobias, blood and needle phobias often involve fainting in the feared situation. Slightly more than half of needle phobias are associated with a history of fainting during injections and blood tests. More than two-thirds of people with blood phobias report a history of fainting upon exposure to blood (Öst, 1992). During these fainting spells, individuals tend to remain unconscious for only a few seconds, although occasionally it can take longer to regain consciousness. After regaining consciousness, it may take from several minutes up to several hours to fully recover and feel normal again.

Why are blood and needle phobias often associated with fainting? Why don't people with other phobias faint? These questions are best answered by considering the survival function of the various sensations that occur during exposure to a dangerous situation. Upon exposure to most dangers (e.g., dangerous animals, oncoming cars), it is most helpful to have a sudden rush of arousal (e.g., racing heart, increased breathing) to increase oxygen flow to the muscles and help the body escape from the danger. This increase in arousal (i.e., the fight-or-flight response) is the typical physical response for most phobias (e.g., animal phobias, height phobias).

Like individuals with other phobias, people with blood and needle phobias frequently report an initial increase in arousal, particularly before entering the feared situation. In fact, they often experience what is called a *diphasic response* (diphasic means "two-part"). During the first phase there is an increase in blood pressure, heart rate, and other signs of arousal. However, during the second phase, which occurs within a few minutes, many individuals with blood and needle phobias experience a sudden drop in heart rate and blood pressure (called a *vasovagal reflex*) that leads to decreased blood flow to the brain and, ultimately, fainting.

There are at least three possible reasons the vasovagal reflex developed in humans. First, in prehistoric times, injured people could escape more easily if they fainted because many wild animals are less likely to attack if their victims are unconscious. Thus, fainting upon injury, or the threat of injury, may have developed to protect people from potential enemies in the wild. A second function of fainting is to promote the development of fear over the possibility of injury. In other words, because people developed a fainting response to situations or objects that might lead to bleeding (e.g., being cut by knives or teeth) and because fainting is unpleasant, people were more likely to learn to fear and avoid these situations and thereby improve their chances of survival in the wild. A third reason fainting may have developed is to prevent excessive blood loss upon injury. Fainting is caused by a sudden drop in blood pressure. Decreased blood pressure also protects an individual from losing too much blood when injured.

Although fainting may be helpful in protecting an individual during an attack or serious injury, it is not helpful to faint when watching a film showing blood or during harmless medical procedures such as receiving injections. Nevertheless, for some people, the fainting response is so strong that it happens even in these perfectly safe situations. It is likely that this fainting response is partially responsible for the development of blood and needle phobias for some individuals. After fainting a few times during medical procedures, it is no wonder people learn to fear these situations. However, about a third of people who faint in medical settings report no fear of these situations, and many people with blood and needle fears report no history of fainting (Kleinknecht & Lenz, 1989). Therefore, fainting does not completely explain the development of blood and needle phobias, and it is possible to fear these situations without ever having fainted. This chapter will discuss strategies for preventing fainting, overcoming fears and phobias of fainting, and overcoming medical and dental fears that are unrelated to fainting.

A Case Example: Needle Phobia

Paul could remember clearly the first time he felt frightened around needles. He was 10 years old and needed a blood test as part of a routine physical. He had never had a blood test before, so he was a bit scared. His mother warned him to look away so it wouldn't hurt as much. Before the blood was drawn, he felt himself getting increasingly scared. His heart was pounding and he felt hot. The doctor could not find a vein in his arm and, after trying several times, switched to the other arm. Paul wiggled and squirmed throughout the procedure and had to be held down by the nurse. When it was finally over, he was in tears. He stood up to leave and became very dizzy. The nurse lay him down until he felt better.

Over the years, Paul's fear worsened. When he was 13, he fainted during a blood test. He received several blood tests throughout high school and passed out about half the time. Paul even noticed that receiving injections began to bother him, although they never had as a child. By the time he graduated from high school, Paul was avoiding all needles whenever possible; in fact, he avoided doctors altogether. Even watching someone receive a shot on television made him feel queasy.

When it came time for Paul to apply to college, he turned down an offer from his first-choice school to avoid the required immunization shots. Despite a strong interest in pursuing a career in medicine, he decided against taking the necessary courses because he couldn't even imagine performing surgery or giving injections. He even put off getting married for more than a year just to avoid a required blood test. He fainted when he finally had the test.

Paul decided it was time to get help when he was offered a job that required a pre-employment blood test. He had two children and was in no position to turn down the job. The potential cost of having his phobia finally seemed too high to ignore. ■

How Common Are Blood, Needle, and Medical Phobias?

About 14% of individuals report a significant fear of blood (Curtis, Magee, Eaton, Wittchen, & Kessler, 1998), and fears of needles, dentists, and related situations are common as well. However, not everyone who fears these situations has a full-blown phobia (including distress or interference in their daily lives). Estimates suggest that 1.6% of individuals have sensations meeting all the criteria for a needle phobia, whereas 2.1% have a phobia of dentists, and 3.3% have an injury phobia (Fredrikson, Annas, Fischer, & Wik, 1996). Blood and needle phobias often run in families. Sixty-one percent of people with blood phobias and 29% of individuals with needle phobias report having a close relative with a similar fear. The tendency for these phobias to run in families is probably related in part to the increased likelihood of fainting upon exposure to blood or needles.

Studies examining sex differences in those suffering from needle phobias have been inconsistent, suggesting that there may be little difference between men and women overall or that blood phobias are slightly more common in women than men. Many individuals have phobias of more than one medical situation. Seventy percent of individuals with blood phobias also fear needles, and about a third of people with needle phobias also fear blood (Öst, 1992). Blood and needle phobias usually begin in childhood, though they can start at any age.

Treatment Strategies

As with all specific phobias, the successful treatment of blood, needle, and other medical phobias involves a variety of components. Most of these components have been discussed in detail in chapters 3 through 7. The remainder of this chapter will discuss specific ways of using these strategies to overcome your phobia. Some additional techniques will be introduced to help you prevent fainting during exposure to blood or needles.

By now, you should have a better understanding of your phobia and may even have a preliminary treatment plan. In chapter 3, you began to identify the specific objects or situations that you fear and whether any of your discomfort is related to phobias over the sensations of fear (e.g., that they may lead you to faint, lose control, be embarrassed, have a heart attack). In addition, you listed your fearful thoughts about your feared situation and you identified some of the obvious and subtle ways that you avoid the situation. Monitoring these fearful reactions will help you plan your treatment and monitor your progress throughout treatment.

This chapter will help you improve and refine your previous observations and monitor your reactions to blood or needles. More-specific instructions will be provided on how to change your fearful thoughts, deal with anxiety over the sensations of fear, prepare for exposure to the feared situation, and carry out the exposure practices.

Refining Your Treatment Plan

Step 1: Identifying Specific Fear Triggers

One of the first steps in overcoming any phobia is to identify the specific triggers for your fear. In chapter 3, you identified the particular situations that you fear. Consider the following list of common triggers for phobias of blood, needles, medical situations, and dentists. Are there any triggers that you would add to your list?

Situations Avoided by People With Phobias of Blood, Needles, Doctors, or Dentists

- Seeing feared situations on television or in movies (e.g., watching surgery, violent films)

- Looking at pictures of injured people (e.g., in newspapers)

- Donating blood, having blood drawn, having a finger-prick blood test

- Visiting a doctor, dentist, or hospital

- Being near someone who is bleeding (e.g., child with a cut)

- Taking certain classes (e.g., medical school, nursing, biology classes involving dissection)

- Watching or playing sports that might involve bleeding (e.g., boxing, hockey, football)

- Looking at needles or at people getting an injection

- Getting injections (e.g., a flu shot) or having an intravenous (IV) needle inserted

- Having blood pressure measured

- Having minor surgery

- Having anesthesia (e.g., at the dentist)

- Handling sharp objects (e.g., knives, razor blades)

- Talking about needles, blood, or medical procedures

- Reading about medical procedures

Phobias take various forms across individuals. The level of discomfort experienced may depend on a wide range of factors. Consider the following list of variables that can affect a person's fear of blood, needles, doctors, or dentists. Do any of these apply to you? Are there any that you would add?

Variables Affecting Fear in People With Phobias of Blood, Needles, Doctors, or Dentists

Blood Phobias

- Type of blood (human vs. animal, self vs. others)

- Form of presentation (seeing real blood vs. seeing blood in photos or movies, or just talking about it)

- Location of exposure (distance from the blood, whether it is seen at home or in the hospital)

- Quantity of blood (bag vs. small vile)

- Presence of injury (a bloody cut vs. menstrual blood)

- Type of injury (scrape vs. deep cut or surgery)

- Duration of exposure

- Alone vs. accompanied by a close friend or relative

Needle Phobias

- Type of needle (for injections, IV, blood draw, finger prick; size of needle)

- Location of needle insertion (arm, mouth, finger, etc.)

- Familiarity with person giving shot

- Form of presentation (getting shot vs. looking at needle or watching injections)

- Training background of person giving injection (e.g., doctor vs. nurse)

- Perceived competence of the person giving the needle

- Location or context of the situation (e.g., doctor's office, blood-donor clinic at work)

- Looking versus not looking at the needle

- Duration of the procedure

- Alone versus accompanied by a close friend or relative

- Amount of pain expected

- Body position (e.g., sitting vs. lying down)

Dental Phobias

- Familiarity with dentist

- Whether nitrous oxide (i.e., laughing gas) or freezing is used

- Type of procedure (e.g., cleaning vs. root canal)

- Amount of stuff (e.g., instruments, cotton) in your mouth during the procedure

- Duration of the procedure

- Amount of pain

- Sound of dentist's drill

- Perceived competence of the dentist and other dental staff

Other Medical Phobias

- Amount of pain experienced

- Probability of being diagnosed with a serious illness

- Type of examination

- Cost of procedures

- Duration of examination or procedure

- Personal nature of problem (e.g., very personal vs. not)

- Having to be naked or partly exposed in front of the doctor

- Type of examination room

- Waiting alone for the doctor to arrive

- Familiarity with the doctor

- Characteristics of the doctor (e.g., sex, age, perceived competence)

Step 2: Identifying Fearful Thoughts

In chapter 3, you began to identify some of your unrealistic beliefs about the situation you fear. As discussed earlier, these beliefs strongly affect whether you will experience fear upon exposure to needles, blood, or other medical situations. For example, if you believe that the dentist will hurt you, you will most likely be fearful at the dentist's office. On the other hand, if you believe that the pain will be manageable, you will be less likely to be afraid. Most people with phobias hold false or exaggerated beliefs about the situation they fear. As a result, they tend to predict that something negative will happen, when in fact it is unlikely to occur. Although many individuals are consciously aware of these fearful predictions, some do not know exactly what it is they are predicting might happen. Because the fear has existed for so long, a person's fearful thoughts may occur very quickly, automatically, and without their awareness. For example, an individual who fears seeing blood might know that seeing blood is not dangerous and might be unaware of any specific negative predictions about what might happen if he or she is exposed to blood. If you are unaware of your fearful predictions about the situation you fear, exposure practices will help make you aware of negative fearful thoughts you didn't even realize you had.

Two broad types of thoughts are relevant in phobias of blood, needles, doctors, and dentists. These include negative predictions about the situation itself and negative predictions about one's reaction to the situation. Negative predictions about the situation may include such thoughts as: (1) the needle will hurt, (2) I will get sick from the needle (e.g., contract AIDS), (3) the needle will break, (4) the doctor or dentist will find something seriously wrong, (5) the doctor, dentist, or nurse will make a mistake (e.g., inject the wrong drug), (6) the doctor or nurse won't be able to find a good vein, and (7) I won't be able to afford the recommended medical or dental treatment. Negative predictions about one's ability to cope may include such thoughts as: (1) I will faint or vomit, (2) I will get so nervous that I will shake and the needle will hurt me, (3) I will embarrass myself, and (4) I will get so fearful I will lose control, go crazy, or die. What sorts of fearful thoughts do you experience? Are there any that you should add to the list you made in chapter 3?

Step 3: Identifying Fearful Behaviors and Avoidance Patterns

An essential step in overcoming a phobia is changing the behavior patterns that maintain the fear. However, to change these patterns, one must first identify them. In chapter 3, you listed some of the subtle and obvious ways in which you avoid blood, needles, or medical procedures. These included refusing to encounter blood or needles; escaping; using distraction; taking medication, alcohol, or drugs; using excessive protection; and relying on superstitious coping strategies.

As discussed earlier, avoidance and escape are effective ways to decrease fear in the short term; however, they contribute to fears and phobias in the long term, meaning that you will become fearful the next time you encounter your phobic object or situation. The reason for this is that avoidance prevents you from learning that what you are most worried about either never or rarely happens, and it prevents you from learning that you can cope with whatever it is you are facing. This learning is critical to the eventual reduction of fears and phobias. To overcome your phobia, it will be essential to resist the urge to avoid the situation that you fear. The first step in this process is to generate lists of situations that you avoid and fearful behaviors that you use when exposed to the situation that you fear. You have already begun this process in earlier chapters. Now, update your list if necessary.

Step 4: Revising Your Exposure Hierarchy

In chapter 6 you developed an *exposure hierarchy* (list of feared situations in order of scariness). Now that you have expanded the list of situations that bring on your fear, and the variables that make the fear better or worse, the next step is to see if you can improve upon your original Exposure Hierarchy.

Step 5: Learning to Cope With and Prevent Fainting

This section is relevant only to individuals with a history of fainting in medical situations. As mentioned earlier, fainting results from a sudden drop in heart rate and blood pressure that leads to a decrease in blood flow to the brain. Although fainting is usually harmless, we suggest that you ask your doctor whether you have any medical conditions that might make it inadvisable to be exposed to situations that could lead to fainting.

Before discussing how to prevent fainting, we will talk about what to do if you faint. Remember that fainting is typically not dangerous. Even if you do nothing, you will most likely regain consciousness within a few seconds. However, there are a few things that can be done to minimize the time you are unconscious and the time it takes to recover. First, it is a good idea to have another person with you during exposure to situations that might lead to fainting. If you faint, this individual can help restore blood flow to the brain more quickly by laying you down on your back and raising your legs. On rare occasions, a person may vomit when unconscious. Being turned on your side will prevent you from choking on vomit.

In the 1980s the psychologist Michael Kozak published two case studies suggesting that tensing all the muscles in the body can prevent fainting by increasing blood pressure in people who fear blood and needles (Kozak & Miller 1985; Kozak & Montgomery, 1981). Building upon these early case reports, the Swedish psychologist Lars-Göran Öst and his colleagues further developed and tested this new treatment for people who faint upon exposure to blood and needles (Öst & Sterner, 1987).

Öst's treatment is very simple and has two main parts. The first part involves learning to tense the main body muscles to increase blood pressure. The second part focuses on learning to notice the early signs of dropping blood pressure. These signs include a variety of sensations, such as light-headedness, and you will begin to notice them earlier with practice. You should begin the tensing exercises when you notice these sensations. Öst called his treatment *applied tension*. The benefit of applied tension is that it can prevent fainting or at least decrease the recovery time from several hours to several minutes if fainting does occur. Even though the technique sounds simple, it takes practice to use it effectively.

Learning to Use Applied Tension

1. Sit in a comfortable chair and tense the muscles of your arms, torso, and legs. Hold the tension for 10 or 15 seconds—long enough to feel warmth or pressure in your head. Release the tension and let your body return to normal for 20 or 30 seconds. Repeat the procedure five times. If you want to see that tensing increases your blood pressure, measure your blood pressure with a home blood-pressure kit before and after tensing.

2. Repeat the first step five times per day (a total of 25 tension cycles per day) for about a week. Practice will help you perfect the technique. If you develop headaches, decrease the strength of your tension or the frequency of your practices.

3. After practicing the tension exercises for a week, start to use the applied tension techniques during your exposure practices as described in the remainder of this chapter. Note, if you are afraid of needles, it is important for you to keep your "needle arm" relaxed during the insertion of the needle. You can incorporate this into your practices by tensing all the muscles except those in one arm.

4. After you can practice exposure with minimal fear and anxiety, discontinue the tension exercises. After the fear has decreased, many individuals are able to be in situations involving blood and needles and not faint. If you still feel faint, begin using the applied tension exercises during exposures again.

Step 6: Consulting Your Physician

Before beginning exposure practices, you should consult your doctor. If you have a history of fainting in the situation that you fear, some of the exposure practices described in this manual may lead to fainting. Although the drop in blood pressure that leads to fainting is usually harmless, you should ask your doctor whether there is any medical reason it might be unsafe for you to faint in these situations. Your physician can tell you if there are any medical circumstances that might make fainting unadvisable for you. For example, if you have a heart condition, your doctor might advise against being in situations that could lead to fainting. However, for most people, as long as you are sitting somewhere where you are unlikely to fall, fainting is not dangerous.

Another reason to consult your physician is to get his or her help creating situations for exposure practices. For example, if you fear medical examinations, you will eventually need to schedule examinations with your physician. It will be helpful for your doctor to understand the reason for your seeking an examination. Similarly, if you fear needles, you will need to practice holding needles, receiving blood tests or injections, and so on. Only a physician can provide these services or give you a proper referral to a medical testing laboratory where these tests can be done. You should explain to your doctor that you are trying to overcome your fear of needles, blood, and so on by exposing yourself to them.

Step 7: Finding the Items Needed for Exposure

Before beginning your exposure practices, spend some time collecting the various things that you may need. As mentioned earlier, you may need someone else to help you with this task in the beginning. For example, if you fear the sight of blood, you can visit bookstores and libraries to find books with pictures that show blood. Medical textbooks are a good place to start. These can be found in your public library, although a better selection is likely to be found in the library or bookstore of a medical school. Also, your doctor may have some graphic photos.

The Internet is also an excellent source of photos. Search Google's Images site (http://images.google.com) using keywords such as "doctors," "surgery," or "operations" for good medical images. For dental images, try keywords such as "dentist," "dental," "dental treatment," "dental tools," and "dentist drill." For blood or needle fears, keywords such as "bloody," "blood," "wound," "surgery," "knife wound," "cut," "needle," "injection," "IV," "syringe," "immunization," "vaccination," or "acupuncture" will bring up all sorts of relevant images. Some of these images may be quite fear-provoking to start with, so you may want to have a friend or helper screen them for you.

In addition to viewing photos, another way of exposing yourself to the situation that you fear is by watching films or television shows that depict surgery, medical procedures, or violence. Violent films are very easy to find in video stores. Surgical films may be more difficult to find, but medical programs are often shown on public television and on some cable channels. For example, consider taping an episode of *ER* or TLC's *The Operation.* Check your local listings. Medical school libraries may have instructional videos to borrow or watch at the library. Also, many popular films (available at your local video store) contain scenes showing medical and dental procedures, injections, and related situations. Ask your friends and family if they know of any. One film with several scenes showing narcotics injections is *Rush,* starring Jason Patric. Other films with injection scenes include *Philadelphia, Drugstore Cowboy, Trainspotting, Dead Man Walking,* and *Panic in Needle Park.* Films with other types of medical scenes include *The Doctor, Patch Adams, Vital Signs,* and *Flatliners.* The films *The Dentist, The Whole Nine Yards,* and *The Secret Lives of Dentists* include scenes depicting dentists.

In addition to looking at pictures and watching films, eventually you will need to be exposed to the real thing. If you fear needles, there are several ways to practice. Finger-prick blood tests can be done at home and won't require the assistance of a physician. Most drug stores sell kits for finger-prick tests for diabetics and other individuals who need to check their blood frequently. The devices that deliver the finger prick are relatively painless and work automatically. Before pricking your finger, clean the area on the finger with an alcohol swab (also available at the pharmacy). Each device may work slightly differently, so read the instructions on the package carefully. You may want to practice the finger-prick tests with your physician or therapist the first time to be sure you are doing it correctly. Be aware that you can prick your fingers repeatedly. Each fingertip can be pricked in the center and on each side. That gives you 30 places (3×10 fingers) to prick your fingertips. Remember, exposure works only if it is done repeatedly. It is not uncommon to feel faint or very fearful the first few times. With practice it will get easier. After your exposure session, dispose of the needles carefully so others aren't pricked accidentally.

Other than finger-prick blood tests, there are few ways people with needle phobias can practice in their own home. Additional exposure practices will require the help of your doctor. Your physician can order some routine blood tests, administer vaccinations, or give saline (a salty fluid that has no affect on the body) injections. Cholesterol tests and "complete blood counts" are commonly used for overcoming these phobias and are practical because they are relatively inexpensive. If you need a vaccination or flu shot, this may be a good time to get it. In addition to contacting your physician, you can contact the Red Cross to donate blood or blood plasma. Talk to your doctor about what sorts of exposure you might set up. Remember, it is better to have several frequent practices. If you need separate blood tests or injections, try to schedule them on different days so you will require more than one needle.

If you fear blood, there are many ways to conduct exposure practices. After you are more comfortable seeing blood in pictures and videos, the next step is to find the real thing. You may use the finger-prick kits described above to make your finger bleed or to make your helper's finger bleed. One of the best practices is to visit places where you are likely to see a lot of blood. Call your local Red Cross to find out where they are having the next blood-donor clinic. Visit the site and just watch for a while. Visit your local hospital. You are likely to find several challenging situations there, including viewing bags of blood at the blood bank.

If you fear dentists, make a dental appointment. Ask to spend extra time in the office sitting in the chair and getting used to being there. If you need several procedures done (check-ups, cleanings, fillings, etc.), schedule them over several visits to get more practice. In fact, it would be advisable to make more appointments than you need (e.g., get a cleaning weekly for a few weeks instead of every six months as is usually recommended). Multiple appointments may be expensive, but you will benefit in the long run. Decreasing your fear of dentists will help you take better care of your teeth and prevent the need for costly procedures in the future.

If you have dental insurance, that will help decrease the cost. Also, routine procedures (e.g., cleanings, check-ups) often are done inexpensively at dental schools and dental-hygiene schools. Although people (especially those with dental phobias) are sometimes nervous about being seen by dental students, there is little risk in having students do these routine procedures. Furthermore, students are closely supervised by their teachers, who are experienced, professional dentists. In addition to the reduced cost, another advantage of practicing at a dental school is that students work more slowly. The slower pace will allow more time for your fears and phobias to decrease.

If you fear other medical situations, think of ways to create them. It would be impractical and unadvisable to overcome a fear of major surgery by having doctors remove organs! However, if you need surgery and are afraid to get it, imaginal exposure may be helpful. Allow yourself to imagine what you might feel. Try to see everything in your imagination that you might see in the real situation. Try to smell the odors of the hospital. Visit hospitals and people who are recovering from surgery. With practice, all these situations will become easier and probably make your own surgery seem less frightening. Remember, it is normal to be nervous before major surgery. Don't expect to be completely calm.

If you fear having your blood pressure measured, consider purchasing a blood-pressure testing kit at a department store, electronics store, or medical supplier. Practice taking your own blood pressure and having someone else take it. When this becomes easier, arrange for a physician or other health care professional to take it.

Step 8: Changing Your Thoughts

In chapter 5 you learned to change some of your unrealistic thoughts and predictions about the situations you fear. Several strategies were discussed. First, you were taught to learn everything that you can about the situation. This can be done in several ways. If you fear needles, ask your doctor what to expect when you get an injection. Find out why it is sometimes difficult to find a vein when having a blood test or giving blood. If this situation frightens you, ask more questions about it. For example, "Does difficulty finding a vein mean that there is something wrong with me?" In most cases, you will be relieved by the answer you get.

If you are afraid of fainting, ask your doctor what happens when a person faints. If you are fearful about visiting the dentist, have your dentist describe everything that he or she is doing. Don't be afraid to ask questions about what to expect. Remember, the more you know about the situation, the more likely you will feel in control and experience less fear.

In addition to asking questions of your doctor or dentist, talk to friends about their experiences. Check the Internet, or visit your local bookstore or library and see what else you can learn. Make a list of questions that you want answered and then set out to get answers.

In chapter 5 you identified instances in which you overestimate and catastrophize. Recall that overestimations refer to exaggerating the likelihood that something bad is going to happen. For example, many people with needle phobias assume that needles hurt more than they do. To counter the tendency to overestimate the probability of something negative occurring, examine the evidence. Ask your friends whether they experience pain during blood tests. Think back to your own experiences with needles. Despite the fear, did they really hurt that much? By examining the evidence, you will decrease the strength of your unrealistic beliefs and thereby decrease your fear.

Catastrophizing refers to exaggerating how bad some event might be if it were to occur. For example, many believe that the pain they will experience at the dentist will be unbearable. It's true that some dental procedures can be painful. However, the pain is usually manageable. Ask yourself what would be so bad about a particular outcome (e.g., "What if I did faint while watching surgery on television?") and how you could cope if what you were most worried about were to come true. For example, how could you cope with an actual faint? Well, you could make sure you were sitting in a comfortable chair to reduce the risk of falling. You could also make sure someone was around in case you fainted. If you did these two things, would fainting really be so bad? In all likelihood, the worst thing that would happen is you would feel the discomfort that you typically feel from your fear. Even the embarrassment would be manageable.

You can practice changing your thoughts before beginning the exposure practices. This will help give you the courage to do the exposure. If you get the urge to escape during a practice, identifying and challenging your thoughts will help you stay in the situation longer.

Step 9: Beginning Exposure Practices

If you have a history of fainting, combine the applied tension techniques described above with all exposure practices. Remember to practice the tension exercises for a full week before beginning exposure. If you do not faint in situations involving blood, needles, doctors, or dentists, practice exposure without using the applied tension strategies.

Chapter 7 describes how to do exposure practices. Exposure sessions should last anywhere from 30 minutes to two hours—for the length of time or the number of repetitions it takes for you to truly learn that whatever you are most worried about never or rarely happens and that you can cope with needles or blood. Of course, the duration of certain types of practices will be beyond your control. For example, an injection rarely takes more than a minute—so in this case it is necessary to practice as many times as is possible. So, if you are practicing pricking your finger with a lancet, be prepared to do it several times. Set aside the time for practices. If you are in a hurry, you will not derive maximum benefit from the session. These sessions will not be easy. If you expect to be able to handle the situation without discomfort, you will be setting yourself up for disappointment. Typically, individuals feel very uncomfortable during the exposure sessions. Some common initial responses include fainting, crying, screaming, and nausea. Early in the treatment, you are likely to experience an increase in negative thoughts or images involving the situation that you fear. You may even experience more nightmares. Many clients report being exhausted after exposure sessions. Others report an increase in overall stress levels, irritability, and a tendency to be startled. These feelings are normal and to be expected; however, they can sometimes lead people to be discouraged and to question whether the treatment is working for them. It may be hard to believe right now, but your fears and phobias will eventually lessen with repeated exposure, and the associated problems will subside as well.

As described in chapter 7, sessions usually begin with easier items from your hierarchy and gradually progress to more difficult items as each step becomes easier. Exposure should be done in a predictable way. Your helper should tell you what each step feels like before you try it. The more prepared you are, the more benefit you will get out of the practices.

If you rent films for exposure practices, remember that you are renting these films not for their entertainment value but rather to overcome your phobia by viewing scenes that you find frightening. In fact, we recommend that you watch scenes showing surgery, blood tests, and injury repeatedly. When viewing these films, rewind the film and watch the difficult scenes several times until you learn that whatever it is you are most worried about doesn't happen or that you can cope with the films as described in chapters 6 and 7.

Allow yourself to feel any discomfort that arises. Don't fight the feelings, and don't interpret them as meaning that you should stop or slow down. You should move through the steps on your hierarchy as quickly as you are willing to. There is no danger in moving too fast and no problem taking a bit longer.

If there are particular aspects of the situation that make it more fearful, introduce these into practices. For example, if just being in a medical setting bothers you, practice being there. Try sitting in the waiting room of the emergency room. If the reminders of the doctor's office make your fear worse, get your helper to wear a white lab coat (if you have one).

To overcome your fear, you may need four or more sessions, although, in some cases, people can get over their fear in only one session. Don't be concerned if it takes you more sessions for the fear to decrease. You will get there in time. Also, to have long-lasting success, it is important to go beyond what you may want to do. For example, most people would not want to prick their fingers up to 10 times. Most people wouldn't want to watch the same surgery scene in a film repeatedly for an hour. However, going beyond what most people would do will make it more likely that the fear won't return.

Troubleshooting

In chapter 7, we provided possible solutions for some of the most common obstacles that arise during exposure-based treatment. Below, we discuss two additional "problems" that may arise in the context of overcoming blood or needle phobias.

Problem: What if I faint?

Solution: You may faint during the exposures. With practice, you will be less likely to faint. If you faint, allow yourself to recover, and start the exposure again. Remember to use the applied-tension strategies. Pay attention to how long you are unconscious. Often it feels like much longer than it actually is.

Problem: I have small veins, so doctors have a lot of trouble getting blood from my arm.

Solution: Some individuals have smaller veins, which can make blood tests more unpleasant and more painful than for most individuals. However, it is still possible that your fears and phobias are out of proportion to the actual danger and pain. You may never learn to enjoy blood tests; however, you can still use the strategies in this chapter to learn to tolerate the pain, just as you can tolerate other types of pain (e.g., headaches, dental treatment). Also, it may be helpful to ask for the most skilled individual to administer your blood test and to warn the person taking your blood of the difficulties you have had in the past because of your small veins.

Homework

✎ Complete the 10 steps discussed in this chapter to overcome your phobia.

✎ Review earlier chapters as necessary—especially chapters 3, 5, and 7. Use the forms and tools presented in these earlier chapters to help you use the strategies discussed in this chapter.

Chapter 9   *Claustrophobia*

Is This Chapter Right for You?

This chapter is for you if you answer *yes* to the following:

1. Do I have an unrealistic or excessive fear of closed-in places?

2. Does the fear cause me distress or interfere with my life? For example, Does it bother me that I have this fear? Do I avoid places or activities because of the fear? Is my lifestyle affected by the fear?

3. Am I motivated to get over my fear?

4. Am I willing to tolerate temporary increases in fears and phobias or discomfort to get over the fear?

What Is Claustrophobia?

Claustrophobia is an *excessive* or *unrealistic* fear of being in closed-in situations. Claustrophobia typically leads to avoidance of these situations and, by definition, must cause significant *distress* or *impairment* in a person's life. For example, if a person fears closed-in places but rarely has reason to be in them, he or she would not be considered phobic. On the other hand, if a mail carrier cannot deliver the mail in office buildings that require he or she use an elevator, this might be diagnosed as a phobia because of the potential interference with his or her work.

Typical situations feared by people with claustrophobia include sitting in the backseat of a two-door car; being in elevators, small rooms (e.g., doctor's examination rooms), or caves; wearing motorcycle helmets; being behind a locked or closed door (e.g., bathroom); taking a shower; using saunas; traveling through tunnels; being hugged; being in closets, even a walk-in closet; being in attics, basements, stairwells, MRI scan machines, or rooms without windows; flying in airplanes; or lying in bed with the covers over his or her head. Of course, most individuals with claustrophobia do not avoid all these situations.

Some people avoid these situations for reasons unrelated to claustrophobia. For example, people with driving phobias might avoid driving through tunnels because they fear traffic accidents. Those with flying phobias avoid flying because they fear crashing. Other people might fear taking showers because of anxiety over being attacked by an intruder or falling in the tub. Individuals with agoraphobia often avoid closed-in places because they fear having a panic attack. However, agoraphobia is also associated with panic attacks in situations other than closed-in places. In contrast to these other phobias, individuals with claustrophobia tend to report a fear of feeling closed-in, restricted, or unable to escape from an enclosed place. In addition, they often report a sense of suffocation when in enclosed situations.

If you fear certain closed-in places for reasons unrelated to the sensation of being closed in, you should read the appropriate chapters in this manual. For example, if you find flying difficult because you fear crashing, then chapter 13 will be helpful. If you fear elevators because of a fear of heights, chapter 11 will be helpful. Remember that people can fear these situations for more than one reason. For example, an individual could fear taking elevators because of anxiety over getting stuck (i.e., claustrophobia) and anxiety over falling (i.e., height phobia). In such a case, we recommend that you read each chapter that is relevant to your phobia (e.g., chapters 9 and 11).

A Case Example: Claustrophobia

■ *Ben was never fearful of enclosed places as a child. He could remember playing in the basement crawl space and hiding in the clothes dryer without feeling frightened. One day, when he was in college, his dormitory elevator became stuck. He pressed the alarm button and waited. Within a few minutes he felt panicky. No help had come and he could feel his heart pounding. It was as if he didn't have enough air to breathe. He felt dizzy and his palms were sweating. He was sure he was going to faint if help didn't arrive soon. About 15 minutes later, the elevator was repaired and he was able to get out. However, he avoided elevators from that time forward.*

Over the years, Ben began to notice that other situations frightened him. On his 21st birthday he planned to go scuba diving with a friend. However, he changed his mind after putting on the mask because he felt he couldn't get enough air. When flying, Ben found that he could be comfortable only on larger airplanes, and, even then, only in aisle seats. Tunnels became increasingly more frightening, and small rooms (e.g., doctor's offices) were very difficult.

Despite his difficulty in these situations, Ben was able to avoid these places without it interfering significantly with his life. It wasn't until he was offered a job on the 30th floor of a large office building that Ben decided he needed treatment for his fear. Without overcoming his fear of elevators, Ben knew it would be very difficult to get to and from his office each day. ■

How Common Is Claustrophobia?

Fears of closed-in places are fairly common, according to a large survey of Americans reported by Curtis, Magee, Eaton, Wittchen, and Kessler (1998). An extreme fear of enclosed places occurs in about 12% of the general population, and just over 4% of people report fear at a level needed for the fear to be considered a phobia. Claustrophobia is more frequently reported by women than by men. It tends to develop relatively late, compared to other specific phobias. The average age of onset for claustrophobia is the early 20s (Öst, 1987), although it can begin at any age.

Treatment Strategies

As with all specific phobias, successful treatment of claustrophobia involves a variety of components, as discussed in chapters 3 through 7. The remainder of this chapter will discuss specific ways of using these strategies to overcome your phobia of closed-in places.

By now, you should have begun to develop an understanding of your phobia and may even have a preliminary treatment plan. In chapter 3, you began to identify the specific situations that you fear. You examined whether any of your discomfort was related to anxiety over the sensations of fear (e.g., that they may lead you to stop breathing, lose control, faint, be embarrassed, have a heart attack). Also, you listed your fearful thoughts concerning enclosed places, and you identified some of the obvious and subtle ways that you avoid these situations. Monitoring your fearful reactions will help you plan your treatment and monitor your progress throughout treatment.

This chapter will help you improve and refine your previous observations and help you monitor your reactions to closed-in places. We will provide more-specific instructions on how to change your fearful thoughts, deal with anxiety over the sensations of fear, prepare for exposure to the feared situation, and carry out the exposure practices.

Refining Your Treatment Plan

Step 1: Identifying Specific Fear Triggers

One of the first steps in overcoming any phobia is to identify the specific triggers for your fear. In chapter 3, you identified the particular situations you fear. Below is a detailed list of situations that people with claustrophobia often fear. Are there any that you would now add to the list you developed earlier?

Places and Situations Often Feared and Avoided by People With Claustrophobia

- Elevators

- Phone booths

- Rooms without windows

- Stairwells, basements, crawl spaces, and attics

- The backseat of a two-door car

- Small rooms (e.g., closet, bathroom, doctor's exam room) with the door shut or locked

- Caves, tents, or tunnels

- Airplanes, crowded railway cars, buses, being below deck on a boat

- Taking a shower or sauna

- Having bed sheets pulled over one's head

- Being hugged

- Wearing a mask (e.g., scuba diving) or motorcycle helmet

- Undergoing an MRI scan

- Using a tanning bed

Note that claustrophobia takes various forms across individuals. The level of discomfort experienced by a specific person may depend on a variety of factors. Below is a list of variables that often affect a claustrophobic individual's fear level. Which of these apply to you? Are there others that you would add to your own list?

Variables Affecting Fear in People With Claustrophobia

- Size of enclosed area

- Presence of windows; amount of light in the area

- Whether mouth and nose are covered (e.g., mask)

- Whether door is closed or locked

- Whether situation can be escaped from easily (e.g., changing room vs. airplane)

- Location in the room (e.g., sitting near the door)

- Presence of other people (e.g., friends, relatives, strangers)

- Duration of exposure

- Temperature and humidity of room (e.g., sauna vs. other room)

- Whether head is covered

- Presence of fresh air

Step 2: Identifying Fearful Thoughts

In chapter 3, you began to identify some of your unrealistic beliefs about closed-in places. As discussed earlier, these beliefs strongly affect whether you will experience fear upon exposure to enclosed situations. For example, if you believe that there is not enough air to breathe in the elevator, it makes sense that you might be more frightened on an elevator than someone who doesn't share that belief. Most individuals hold false beliefs about the situations they fear. As a result, they often make negative predictions about events that are unlikely to occur. Although many people with claustrophobia are consciously aware of these fearful predictions, some do not know exactly what it is that they are predicting might happen. Because the fear has existed for so long, a person's fearful thoughts may occur very quickly, automatically, and without their awareness. For example, you might fear being in the backseat of a two-door car but be unsure why the situation frightens you. If you are unaware of your fearful thoughts about the situation you fear, exposure practices will help make you aware of thoughts that you didn't even realize you had.

Fears of closed-in places are usually associated with two main types of fearful predictions—not being able to escape and running out of air. In addition, you may find that other types of negative thoughts run though your head, including fearful thoughts about your own reactions in the situation; for example, you may believe your fears and phobias will lead you to faint, suffocate, lose control, be embarrassed, or die.

Step 3: Identifying Fearful Behaviors and Avoidance Patterns

An essential step in overcoming a phobia is changing the behavior patterns that maintain the fear. In chapter 3, you listed some of the ways in which you avoid facing feared situations, including refusing to encounter closed-in places, escaping, using distraction, using excessive protection, over-relying on safety signals, and using medication, alcohol, or drugs. As discussed earlier, avoidance and escape are effective ways to decrease fear in the short term; however, they contribute to fears and phobias in the long term, meaning that you will become fearful the next time you encounter your phobic object or situation. The reason for this is that avoidance prevents you from learning that what you are most worried about either never or rarely happens, and it prevents you from learning that you can cope with whatever it is you are facing. This learning is critical to the eventual reduction of fears and phobias. To overcome your phobia, it is essential to resist the urge to avoid the situation you fear. The first step in this process is to generate lists of situations that you avoid and fearful behaviors that you use when exposed to the situation that you fear. You have already begun this process in earlier chapters. Now, update your list if necessary.

Step 4: Revising Your Exposure Hierarchy

In chapter 6 you developed an *exposure hierarchy* (list of feared situations, ranked by scariness). Now that you have expanded the list of situations that bring on your fear, and the variables that make the fear stronger or weaker, the next step is to see if you can improve your Exposure Hierarchy by adding or deleting items based on information gained from this chapter.

Step 5: Finding the Situations Needed for Exposure

Before beginning your exposure practices, it is important to take some time to think of places to practice. There are many places to find the situations that you fear. Ask your friends and relatives for ideas. They may know of places in your neighborhood where you can practice.

If you fear driving through tunnels, find out where there are tunnels in your area. Find out how they compare, with respect to length, darkness, traffic, and other factors that may affect your level of fearfulness. If caves bother you, ask people you know where you might find caves nearby. Certain amusement parks may have rides that require people to be enclosed (e.g., Ferris wheels with enclosed seats).

There are probably a variety of situations that you can create at home for practicing. For example, a bathroom with no windows is a great practice situation for many people with claustrophobia. Try being in the bathroom with the door closed. When that becomes easier, lock the door. After you are more comfortable with the door locked, switch the lock so that the room locks from the outside. In other words, remove the lock and door-knob and reinstall them backward, so that when the door is locked, you cannot get out of the room. Arrange for a family member or friend to let you out after a specified time. As you can see, a single room can be used for practices of varying levels of difficulty.

Other places to practice in the home include closets, crawl spaces, and attics. Objects that might be helpful for practices include things that you might wear over your head (motorcycle helmets, masks, paper bags, pillowcases, bed sheets, sleeping bags, helmet-style hair dryers, etc.). Of course, use caution when covering your head (e.g., don't use plastic bags!).

Other places to practice include small cars, phone booths, department store changing rooms, elevators, saunas, small tents, and crowded places. If flying in small airplanes bothers you, arrange to take a short flight. If being hugged makes you feel closed-in, find someone with whom you feel comfortable practicing hugging.

For each of these situations you think might be difficult, make a list of places where you could obtain the objects that you need. In addition, include specific locations where you can practice. If you run out of ideas, ask others for suggestions.

Step 6: Changing Your Thoughts

In chapter 5 you learned to change some of your unrealistic thoughts and predictions. You were encouraged to learn everything you can about the situation. This can be done in several ways. If you are afraid that you will be unable to breathe with your head under the covers, watch someone else do it first. Or put part of the pillowcase over your mouth and test whether you can breathe. If you fear elevators, learn what you can about elevators, their mechanics, and why they are unlikely to get stuck forever. Remember, the more you know about the situation you fear, the more likely you will feel in control and experience less fear.

Also, in chapter 5 you identified instances in which you use overestimations and catastrophizing. Recall that overestimations refer to when you exaggerate the likelihood that something bad is going to happen. For example, many people with claustrophobia believe that they will not be able to breathe in a closed-in situation, despite the fact that it is impossible to run out of air in most closed-in situations. To counter the tendency to overestimate the probability that something bad will occur, examine the evidence. For example, if you fear that you will get stuck in an elevator, consider the realistic probabilities. Although it is true that people occasionally get stuck in elevators, the vast majority of people do not. Consider all the people that you know and the number of times each of them rides elevators in a given year. How many of these elevator rides has led to someone getting stuck? Probably very few, if any. If you do hear of someone getting stuck in an elevator, remember to consider the millions of other people who don't get stuck each day. Furthermore, if you fear suffocating in a stuck elevator, consider the realistic probability of that happening. It is unlikely that you would be able to think of any instance of a person ever suffocating in an elevator. How realistic is it to assume that you will be the first person ever to run out of air in an elevator? By examining the evidence, you will decrease the strength of your unrealistic beliefs and thereby decrease your fear.

Catastrophizing refers to an exaggeration of how bad some event might be if it were to occur. For example, many people with claustrophobia believe that it would be unbearable to be stuck in an elevator. It's normal not to want to be stuck in an elevator, but would it really be that bad? Would you really die, go crazy, lose control, or suffocate?

Ask yourself what would be so bad about a particular outcome (e.g., "What if someone noticed that I was scared?") and how you could cope if what you were most worried about were to come true. For example, what might actually happen if you got stuck in an elevator? Can you think of anyone that you know who has been stuck in an elevator? How did he or she cope with it? Did he or she eventually get out safely? How could you cope with getting stuck in an elevator? Realistically, what's the worst thing that might happen? In all likelihood, the worst thing that would happen is that you would feel the extreme discomfort that you typically feel from your fear. You have managed to survive when feeling frightened in the past. There is no reason to believe that you wouldn't survive the next time if you were stuck in a closed-in place.

You can practice changing thoughts before the exposure practice begins. This will help give you the courage to do the exposure. If you get the urge to escape during a practice, identifying and challenging your irrational thoughts will help you stay in the situation longer.

Step 7: Beginning Exposure Practices

In chapter 7, you learned how to do exposure practices. You learned that practices should be prolonged (at least 30 minutes, but ideally even longer), frequent (at least three to four times per week), and predictable, with as few surprises as possible. Sessions should begin with easier items and gradually progress to more difficult items as each step becomes easier. After your practices have become easier, you should introduce more difficult or unexpected conditions to the situation. For example, you or your helper could press the button to purposely stop the elevator, close the closet door while you are inside, and so on. The rate at which you move to more difficult items is up to you. The sooner you try the more difficult steps, the faster you will overcome your fear.

Don't expect the practices to be easy. Typically, individuals feel very uncomfortable during the exposure sessions. Crying, screaming, shaking, and panic are common responses at first. Early in the treatment, you may experience an increase in your anxiety even when you are not in the feared situation. You may also feel exhausted after exposure sessions.

These feelings are normal and to be expected; however, they can sometimes lead people to be discouraged and to question whether the treatment is working for them. Contrary to what you might expect, these negative feelings are a sign that treatment is working. It is these feelings that have kept you avoiding the situation for so long. After the initial period of increased distress, you will eventually feel more comfortable.

Step 8: Dealing With Your Fear of Sensations

As mentioned in chapter 3, many people experience anxiety over the fear sensations that they feel in closed-in places. For example, individuals sometimes believe that a breathless feeling might lead to suffocating or passing out. Also, certain sensations can be misinterpreted as signs that a person will lose control, have a heart attack, embarrass themselves, vomit, or faint. If you don't fear these sensations, it is not necessary to work on overcoming such a fear and you can skip this section.

However, if the sensations bother you, two main strategies will be useful: cognitive therapy and exposure. First, use the cognitive strategies discussed in chapter 5. Identify the predictions that you are making and examine the evidence for these predictions. For example, if you believe that your dizziness might lead to fainting, examine the evidence. Have you ever fainted in a closed-in place before? Have you ever heard of anyone fainting in a closed-in place? What is the realistic probability that this will happen today? You can counter your catastrophic thoughts about the sensations in a similar way. For example, if you believe people seeing you shake would be awful, try asking yourself, "What would be so awful about it, other than the temporary feeling of embarrassment? How could I deal with the situation if it did happen?"

The second strategy for overcoming your fear of sensations is to deliberately bring on these sensations in the very situation that you fear. After being in the situation becomes easier, use the sensation exercises discussed in chapter 7 to increase the intensity of the sensations you fear while in the enclosed space. For example, after you become more comfortable sitting in a closet, try wearing a heavy sweater to make yourself feel hot or try taking a few fast and deep breaths to feel dizzy or short of breath. This will help you learn that the sensations are not dangerous. Of course, if you have any medical problems (e.g., heart condition, asthma, epilepsy), remember to check with your doctor before doing the exercises described in chapter 7.

Homework

✎ Complete the eight steps discussed in this chapter to overcome your phobia.

✎ Review earlier chapters as necessary—especially chapters 3, 5, and 7. Use the tools presented in those chapters to help you use the strategies discussed in this chapter.

Chapter 10

Animal and Insect Phobias

Is This Chapter Right for You?

This chapter is for you if you answer yes to the following:

1. Do I have an unrealistic or excessive fear of an animal or insect?

2. Does the fear cause me distress or interfere with my life? For example, Does it bother me that I have this fear? Do I avoid places or activities because of the fear? Is my lifestyle affected by the fear?

3. Am I motivated to get over my fear?

4. Am I willing to tolerate temporary increases in fears and phobias or discomfort to get over my fear?

What Is an Animal Phobia?

An animal phobia is an excessive or unrealistic fear of a specific animal and typically leads one to avoid situations where the animal is likely to be found. The fear must cause significant distress or impairment in a person's life before it can be called a phobia. For example, a person who fears harmless spiders and lives in an area where spiders are rarely found might not be considered phobic because this fear would not interfere with the person's functioning, and it would probably not bother the individual to have the fear. For a fear to be called a phobia, it must be excessive, interfere with a person's life, or cause distress.

Although people can have a phobia of any animal, the most common animals feared in North America are snakes, spiders, bees, other insects, dogs, cats, birds, mice, rats, and bats. The environment or location where an individual lives may affect the types of fears that he or she develops. For example, an individual who fears snakes might be more likely to have a snake phobia if he or she lives in a desert area, where snakes are plentiful, as opposed to the city, where snakes are rarely encountered.

Like other phobias, animal phobias are associated with extreme fear. However, people with certain types of animal phobia (especially phobias of bugs, spiders, snakes, mice, and other "creepy-crawly creatures") also tend to experience disgust when exposed to the animals they fear, either in real life, or in images (e.g., video, photos). In fact, for some people, disgust is even stronger than fear. Fortunately, the strategies described in this workbook (especially the exposure-based strategies) usually help decrease levels of both disgust and fear. Treatment seems to work well, regardless of whether the primary emotion is disgust, fear, or a combination of the two.

A Case Example: Dog Phobia

■ *Max never had a problem with dogs as a young child. In fact, his family had a basset hound when he was growing up, and he had no fear of the family dog. One day, when Max was about 10 years old, he was playing with his younger brother in their next-door neighbor's back yard when he suddenly heard loud barking and turned around to see the neighbor's German shepherd charging at him. He and his brother ran as quickly as they could. The dog was tied to the front porch, so they managed to get away without being bitten.*

From that day on, Max noticed that he was more careful when walking by that neighbor's house. He tended to stay away from that yard and even refused to go to his neighbor's birthday party that year. When walking on his street, Max tried to keep to the other side of the road. He rarely encountered other dogs, and his fear was more or less limited to large dogs.

Several years later, Max was visiting a friend who owned a small terrier. He bent down to pet the dog while it was eating; the dog bit Max. From that time on, Max avoided all dogs except his own. When he saw a dog on the street, he panicked and would run to the other side of the street. His heart would race, and he felt faint and sweaty. His shaking was so intense that he sometimes thought he might fall down. In fact, he often had his family check outside for dogs before he left the house. He started to avoid pet stores and also avoided visiting friends until after he had asked if they owned dogs or not. Interestingly, he never developed a fear of his own basset hound, even though the dog had bitten him several times over the years. Max eventually decided to seek treatment when he couldn't visit his fiancée's home because she owned a dog. ■

How Common Are Animal Phobias?

About 22% of people in the United States have an extreme animal fear, and about 5.7% of the population has a fear that is severe enough to be considered a phobia (Curtis, Magee, Eaton, Wittchen, & Kessler, 1998). This makes animal phobias the most prevalent of all specific phobias. Among people with animal phobias, the most commonly feared animals are snakes, spiders, bugs, rodents, and other creepy-crawlies (Bourdon et al., 1988). Animal phobias tend to develop very early in life, often before the age of 10, although many individuals report that their fear began in adulthood, while others do not recall any specific onset and report having had the fear all their lives. About three-quarters of individuals with animal phobias are women.

Treatment Strategies

As with all specific phobias, successful treatment of animal phobias involves a variety of components. These components were discussed in detail in chapters 3 through 7. The rest of this chapter will discuss how to use these strategies to overcome your animal phobia.

By now, you should have begun to develop an understanding of your phobia and may even have a preliminary treatment plan. In chapter 3, you began to identify the specific objects or situations that you fear. You also examined whether any of your discomfort was related to the sensations of fear (e.g., that they might lead you to lose control, be embarrassed, have a heart attack). You also listed fearful thoughts concerning your feared animal and identified some of the obvious and subtle ways that you avoid the animal. Having monitored the situations that trigger your fear and recorded your fearful thoughts and behaviors, you will find it easier to develop a treatment plan and monitor your progress during treatment.

This chapter will help you improve and refine your previous observations and the monitoring of your animal phobia. Also, we will provide more-specific instructions on how to change your fearful thoughts, deal with the sensations of fear, prepare for exposure to the feared animal, and, finally, carry out the exposure practices.

Step 1: Identifying Specific Fear Triggers

One of the first steps in overcoming an animal phobia is identifying the specific triggers for your fear. For example, below is a list of situations that an individual with a bird phobia might avoid. Take a look at the list. Are there any triggers or situations relevant to your fear that you should add to your own list?

Situations Often Feared and Avoided by People With a Bird Phobia

■ Being near the bird department in a pet store

■ Leaving the house in the morning on summer days

■ Being in a park or near trees where there are birds

■ Visiting the bird area at the zoo

■ Visiting a beach where there might be seagulls

■ Visiting people who own pet birds

■ Walking under bridges or eating on outdoor patios (where there may be birds)

■ Standing near a large flock of birds

■ Listening to birds chirping in the morning

■ Being in the same room as a bird in a cage

■ Being in the same room as an uncaged bird

■ Touching a bird

■ Feeding the ducks at a nearby pond

Of course, each person experiences his or her animal phobia differently. There are many factors that can affect a person's level of fear in the presence of their feared animal. On the next page is a list of such variables. Which of these apply to your fear?

Variables Affecting Fear in People With Animal Phobias

- Physical features (e.g., shape, color, size, hairiness)

- Potential for being bitten

- Whether another person is present

- Location of animal (e.g., a spider in my backyard vs. in my bed)

- Whether the animal is restrained (e.g., dog on a leash vs. loose)

- Form of exposure (e.g., imagining snakes, talking about snakes, or seeing cartoon pictures of snakes, toy snakes, photos of snakes, videotaped snakes as opposed to live snakes)

- Distance from animal (e.g., standing across the room from a cat, standing a few feet behind a cat, standing directly in front of a cat, touching the cat while wearing gloves, touching a cat without gloves, having a cat sit on your lap)

- Type of movement (e.g., speed, unpredictability, jumping)

Step 2: Identifying Fearful Thoughts

In chapter 3, you began to identify some of your unrealistic beliefs about the animal that you fear. As discussed earlier, these beliefs strongly affect whether you will experience fear upon exposure to the animal. For example, if you believe that a bird might attack you, it follows that you will be frightened around birds. On the other hand, if you believed that birds were likely to fly away as you approached them, you might be less likely to be afraid. Most people with animal phobias hold false or exaggerated beliefs about the animal they fear. As a result, they tend to predict that something negative will happen, when in fact that is unlikely. Although many individuals are consciously aware of these fearful predictions, some do not know exactly what it is they think might happen. Because the fear has existed for so long, a person's fearful thoughts may occur very quickly, automatically, and without awareness. For example, most individuals who fear worms know that worms are not dangerous and are unaware of any specific negative predictions about what a worm might do to them. If you are unaware of your fearful predictions about the animal you fear, exposure practices will help make you aware of negative fearful thoughts you didn't even realize you had.

Usually, fearful thoughts about animals are focused on the possibility of the animal doing something unpleasant or dangerous. Typical predictions may include (1) the animal will move toward me, (2) the animal will jump on me, (3) the animal will crawl on me, (4) the animal will bite or attack me, (5) the animal will make me sick or dirty, and (6) the animal can tell I am afraid. In addition, some people with animal phobias report anxiety over the possibility of something bad happening as a result of the intense anxiety or physical sensations they feel. For example, they might fear throwing up, fainting, losing control, embarrassing themselves, or even dying. What are your anxiety-provoking thoughts about your feared animal?

Step 3: Identifying Fearful Behaviors and Avoidance Patterns

An essential step in overcoming a phobia is changing the behaviors that maintain the fear. Types of subtle and obvious avoidance were discussed in previous chapters. In chapter 3, you listed ways in which you avoid your feared animal, including refusing to approach the animal, escaping, using distraction, using excessive protection, relying on safety signals, and using medication, alcohol, or drugs.

In an effort to protect themselves from unexpected encounters with the feared animal, many individuals check excessively to make sure that the animal is not nearby. For example, people with spider phobias may check their cars before getting in or might look behind doors before entering rooms and examine closets before reaching in. Individuals with fears of dogs, cats, or birds often check the area outside their houses before leaving home or have a family member do so. Likewise, people with snake phobias may ask friends to warn them about films that contain scenes with snakes.

As discussed earlier, avoidance and escape are effective ways to decrease fear in the short term; however, they contribute to fears and phobias in the long term, meaning that you will become fearful the next time you encounter your phobic object or situation. The reason for this is that avoidance prevents you from learning that what you are most worried about either never or rarely happens, and it prevents you from learning that you can cope with whatever it is you are facing. This learning is critical to the eventual reduction of fears and phobias. To overcome your phobia, it is essential to resist the urge to avoid the situation you fear. The first step in this process is to generate lists of situations you avoid and fearful behaviors you use when exposed to the situation you fear. You have began this process in earlier chapters. Now, update your list if necessary.

Fearful Behaviors in People With Dog Phobias

- Avoiding watching movies about dogs

- Avoiding walking alone around the neighborhood

- Avoiding walking by or visiting pet stores

- Avoiding visiting parents, who have two dogs

- Avoiding speaking with Frank, who seems to talk continuously about his dogs

- Avoiding walking past Toyland, where there is a large stuffed St. Bernard in the window

- Avoiding buying a dog, even though the family wants one

- Avoiding visiting friends who have dogs

- Changing the channel when a dog is shown on TV

- Crossing the street if a dog is nearby

- Wearing extra layers of clothing for protection from possible dog bites

- Carrying "pepper spray" in case a dog gets too close

- Avoiding living in an apartment complex that accepts dogs

- Asking friends if they have dogs before visiting

- Having someone else check outside for dogs before leaving the house

Step 4: Revising Your Exposure Hierarchy

In chapter 6, you developed an *exposure hierarchy* (list of feared situations ranked from easiest to hardest). Now that you have expanded the list of situations you avoid, those that cause you fear, and the variables that make the fear better or worse, the next step is to update your Exposure Hierarchy.

Use the information you have compiled as you have read through this chapter to revise your exposure hierarchy if necessary.

Step 5: Finding the Items Needed for Exposure

Before beginning your exposure, spend some time collecting the various items (e.g., animals, pictures, containers) you will need. As mentioned earlier, you may need someone else to help you with this task at first. You or your helper should visit bookstores and libraries to find books with relevant pictures and information. Alternatively, you can check out Google's Images site at http://images.google.com, and search for your feared animal (e.g., dogs, spiders, mice).

You can also rent or purchase films with scenes involving the feared animal. Here are just a few examples:

- Spiders: *Spider Man, Charlotte's Web*

- Snakes: *Raiders of the Lost Ark*

- Insects: *Microcosmos, Patch Adams* (butterfly), *Joe's Apartment* (cockroaches)

- Birds: *Winged Migration*

- Dogs: *Benji, Lassie, 101 Dalmations, Best in Show*

- Cats: *Men in Black, The Adventures of Milo and Otis*

You may also consider purchasing nature videos about the animal you fear. A couple of Internet sites that sell videos featuring such animals include http://naturepavilion.com and http://shop.nationalgeographic.com. Consider borrowing or buying toy replicas of the animal you fear. For example, some toy stores and nature shops have fairly realistic toy snakes. Ask your friends if they have seen any realistic rubber snakes recently, and visit the stores where these artificial snakes are sold. Field guides are a good source for information on and graphic pictures of the animal you fear. The Audubon Society publishes field guides with photographs of reptiles, insects, spiders, birds, and other animals (http://www.audubon.org/market/licensed/field guides.html). Golden publishes a less expensive field guide with drawings instead of photographs. Also, there are a variety of inexpensive children's books with large photographs of snakes, spiders, birds, dogs, and almost every other animal that one might fear.

If any of the items mentioned frightens you, it may be useful to buy or borrow them. However, if pictures and toys do not bother you, there is no reason to obtain them. It is necessary to practice exposure only to situations that you find frightening. Similarly, if you are willing to start your exposures using real animals, there is no need to practice with toys, photos, and videos. It is fine to start with the real thing.

Real animals can be found in a variety of places. If you fear snakes, you might find them at zoos or pet stores, or through people with pet snakes. Ask friends if they know anyone who owns a snake and might be willing to help; if not, ask around at pet stores. Although some stores may refuse to help, others may be willing to spend time with you on a slow day, showing you how to handle snakes and allowing you to handle them. If nothing else, you should be able to look at the snakes in the glass aquariums at pet stores and zoos. It may take some creativity to come up with ways to find live snakes that you can handle. Friends, relatives, acquaintances, and others may know of places in town with snakes or of people who own snakes.

If you fear spiders, good places to find them include basements, garages, and other dark places. Ask your friends to start catching them for you. After spiders are caught they should be placed in a covered jar or cup with tiny air holes. Putting a small piece of moist paper towel in the jar will help keep the spider alive longer.

Other animals (e.g., birds, mice, dogs, cats) can be found in pet stores and through pet owners. There are good places to find these animals outside as well (e.g., parks, beaches, fields, in the neighborhood). Take some time to ask others for suggestions about all the places where you might find the animal you fear. Make a list of these places and begin arranging to gather some of the items and animals you need. Remember, if you don't fear something (e.g., pictures), there is no need to spend time and money finding it. Your efforts should focus on finding the things you fear.

It is helpful to find animals of different types. For example, when working with spider phobias, we tend to use spiders of various sizes, shapes, and speeds. Hierarchies are created taking into account the different types of spiders available. For example, clients might begin with smaller spiders and work their way up to larger, scarier spiders.

Remember to use caution. Animal fears are not always irrational. For example, some areas of the country have poisonous snakes in the wild. Do not approach any animal too closely unless you know something about it. Before handling a pet, ask the owner how the animal prefers to be handled. In all the years that we have treated animal phobias, we have never heard of a client get bitten or hurt during exposure practices. Nevertheless, it is appropriate to exercise some caution around unfamiliar animals. For example, although it is probably safe to feed pigeons in the park, it is unadvisable to try to pick up a bird in the wild. In contrast, many pet birds are comfortable being handled. If you are afraid of spiders and live in an area with poisonous spiders, it would be wise to use a field guide to identify the area's spiders before handling them (particularly if they are not the typical spiders found in your home).

Step 6: Changing Your Thoughts

In chapter 5 you learned to change some of your unrealistic thoughts and predictions about the animal you fear. Several strategies were discussed. First, you were asked to learn everything you can about the animal you fear. This can be done in several ways. A library, bookstore, or pet store is a good place to start. Look through books about the animal you fear. Pet store employees and pet owners can also be good sources of information. Make a list of questions you want answered and then set out to get answers from these sources. Here are some examples of questions you might ask in the case of a snake phobia:

- Do most snakes bite? Do they even have teeth? Are some more likely to bite than others? Which snakes are harmless? Under what conditions is a snake likely to bite?

- What does it feel like to be bitten by a snake? What could I do if I were bitten by a nonpoisonous snake? What about a poisonous snake?

- How do snakes like to be handled? What does it feel like to hold a snake?

- Why do snakes move the way they do?

- Why do snakes stick out their tongues? Does that mean they are going to bite?

- Do snakes carry and spread diseases?

- Is a snake likely to crawl on me in the wild?

- Can a snake strangle me? How likely is that?

In chapter 5 you identified instances when you engage in negative thought patterns such as *probability overestimating* and *catastrophizing*. Recall that an overestimation is when you exaggerate the likelihood that something bad is going to happen (e.g., that a snake will attack). To counter this tendency, examine the evidence. Ask your friends what percentage of their encounters with dogs led to being bitten. By examining the evidence, you will decrease the strength of your unrealistic beliefs and thereby decrease your fear.

Catastrophizing is when you exaggerate how bad an event might be if it did occur. For example, people who fear spiders often assume it would be "terrible" if a harmless spider were to crawl on them. Ask yourself "What would be so bad about that? What would happen if a harmless spider crawled on me?" and consider how you could cope if it actually happened. Usually spiders do not crawl on people. However, sometimes they do. What could you do if a harmless spider crawled on you? Well, one thing you could do is nothing. Let the spider crawl on you and see what happens. See if you can control where it crawls by placing a hand in front of it. See how it feels. It will probably feel like an ant or some other bug. What if it becomes uncomfortable? Well, then you could brush it off, the way you would an ant. In other words, don't stop at the thought, "it would be awful," and don't assume that that thought is true. Let yourself think ahead to how you can deal with the situation. Probably the worst thing you will experience is extreme discomfort. With practice, the discomfort will decrease significantly.

Step 7: Beginning Exposure Practices

Chapter 7 describes how to do exposure practices. Exposure sessions should last anywhere from 30 minutes to 2 hours. Set aside the time in advance. If you are in a hurry, you will not derive maximum benefit from the session. Plan to stay in the situation long enough to learn that what you are most worried about never or rarely happens or that you can cope with facing the animal that has bothered you up until now.

Typically, individuals feel very uncomfortable during the exposure sessions. Some common initial responses include crying, screaming, feeling nauseated, and panicking. Early in the treatment, you are likely to experience an increase in negative thoughts or images involving the animal you fear. You may even have more nightmares. Many clients report being exhausted after exposure sessions. Others report increased stress levels, irritability, and a tendency to be startled. These feelings are normal and will improve as your treatment progresses.

As described in chapter 7, select easier items from your hierarchy when you first start exposure sessions, and as each step becomes easier, gradually progress to more difficult items. When you start working with the live animal, begin with the animal restrained. For example, your helper should hold the dog on a leash. Likewise, spiders should be in a large clear container (e.g., a plastic tub). At first, your helper will need to ensure that the animal does not get loose. Eventually you will be able to handle the animal.

If you are working with spiders, a first step might be learning to catch the spider by lowering a jar over it and sliding a card under the jar to trap it. Once you learn to capture the spiders yourself, you will no longer need your helper to catch them for you. The next step might be gently touching the spider with a pencil and eventually with your hand. You will get used to the feeling of spider webs on your hands. You will also get used to the feeling of the spider moving and trying to jump off your hands.

Likewise, if you are working with other animals, try to begin with easier items from your hierarchy. For example, if it is easier to touch the tail of a dog than its face, begin with the tail. Gradually move your hands closer to its face as each step becomes easier.

Exposure should be done in a predictable way. Your helper should tell you what it feels like to handle the animal before you actually touch it. Your helper should never place the animal on or near you without first getting your permission. Making each step in the session predictable and keeping it under your control will make it much easier for your fear to decrease.

Allow yourself to feel any discomfort that arises. Don't fight the feelings, and don't interpret them as meaning that you should stop or slow down. Move through the steps on the hierarchy as quickly as you are willing to. There is no danger in moving too fast. It is OK to skip steps and change your hierarchy as you go along. However, before moving to a more difficult task, you should repeat a step until your fear decreases.

To overcome your fear, you may need four or more sessions, each lasting up to three hours, although, in many cases, people with animal phobias are able to overcome their fear in one long session. Don't worry if you need more sessions for the fear to decrease; you will get there in time. In addition, to have long-lasting success, it is important to go beyond what you may want to do. For example, we often help people with spider phobias reach a point where they can comfortably have a spider crawl on their hands, arms, stomach, and face. Individuals with dog phobias should reach a point at which they can open a dog's mouth and touch its teeth (providing the owner says the dog doesn't mind people doing this). "Overdoing it" will make the smaller steps seem even easier and will make it more likely that the fear won't return. Of course, don't practice anything that most people would consider dangerous.

If there are particular aspects of the animal's behavior that bother you, work on getting the animal to do these things. For example, if it bothers you when a spider moves, try to get it to move. If it bothers you when a dog gets excited, try to get it excited by throwing a ball or trying to play with it. If the movement of a snake's tongue frightens you, pay extra attention to these movements. If the fluttering of a bird's wings scares you, try to get the bird to fly. Pay attention to the behaviors that bother you and attempt to learn more about the functions of these behaviors.

You can try to change your thoughts before beginning the exposure. Changing your negative thoughts will help give you the courage to get closer to the animal. In addition, identifying and challenging your irrational thoughts may help you stay in the exposure situation longer, even when you want to escape.

Troubleshooting

In chapter 7, we provided possible solutions for some of the most common obstacles that arise during exposure-based treatment. Below, we discuss "problems" that may arise in the context of overcoming an animal phobia.

Problem: The animal suddenly moves toward me unexpectedly.

Solution: Animals may surprise you sometimes. Spiders may jump a few inches or spin threads on your hands. Dogs may approach you quickly to smell you. Snakes may suddenly move after remaining still for some time. Anticipate sudden movements. Expect the unexpected (like they teach in defensive driving courses). Decide in advance how you will handle such an event. However, no matter how prepared you are, you may still unintentionally move back from the animal or even drop it. If you are holding an animal that you might drop, have a container under the animal to catch it. If you drop it or move away, resume contact with the animal as soon as possible.

Problem: My fear is too intense for me to approach the animal.

Solution: Use the cognitive countering strategies to identify and change your fearful thoughts. Also, move to a lower item on your hierarchy. For example, if the birds in your local pet store are too big to look at, find a store with smaller birds. If you can't touch the front of the spider, touch the back. If you can't touch the spider with your hand, use a pencil at first. You get the idea. Do what you can do. The harder steps will eventually get easier. A few other ideas: Spend more time watching your helper do the things you fear. As you do so, your fear will become more manageable. Remind yourself that it is normal and even necessary for you to feel discomfort. Finally, if it's just too uncomfortable, take a short break and come back to it later. However, before you take a break, decide exactly when you will resume your practice.

Problem: I get really "grossed out" during exposures.

Solution: That's OK. You will be less "grossed out" over time. If you think you might vomit, have a bucket in the room. It is important to practice the exposure regardless of the discomfort.

Homework

✎ Complete the eight steps discussed in this chapter to overcome your phobia.

✎ Review earlier chapters as necessary—especially chapters 3, 5, and 7. Use the forms and tools presented in these earlier chapters to help you use the strategies discussed in this chapter.

Chapter 11

Height Phobia

Is This Chapter Right for You?

This chapter is for you if you answer *yes* to the following:

1. Do I have an unrealistic or excessive fear of high places?

2. Does the fear cause me distress or interfere with my life? For example, Does it bother me that I have this fear? Do I avoid places or activities because of the fear? Is my lifestyle affected by the fear?

3. Am I motivated to get over my fear?

4. Am I willing to tolerate temporary increases in fears and phobias or discomfort to get over my fear?

What Is a Height Phobia?

A height phobia (also called *acrophobia*) is an excessive or unrealistic fear of being in situations that involve heights. A height phobia typically leads to avoidance of high places and, by definition, must cause significant distress or impairment in a person's life. For example, if a person fears heights but rarely has reason to be in a high place, he or she would not be considered phobic. On the other hand, an individual who drives for a living but avoids crossing bridges or elevated roads might be diagnosed with a phobia because of the potential interference with his or her work.

Typical situations feared by height-phobic individuals include using ladders, being on rooftops, standing on chairs or desks (e.g., to hang a picture), walking or driving over bridges, driving on elevated highways, standing near a high railing, hiking, skiing, using chair lifts, flying, using escalators, being in a glass elevator, ascending tall buildings, watching movies with scenes involving heights, using fire escapes, being on balconies, sitting in high theater seats, visiting overlooks, and encountering just about any other high place. Of course, most individuals with height phobias do not avoid all these situations.

Also, a person who avoids these situations for reasons unrelated to a fear of heights (e.g., fear of crashing in an airplane, fear of getting stuck in an elevator) wouldn't be considered height phobic. If you fear driving in high places or flying in airplanes, you should also read chapters 12 or 13 of this manual. Chapter 12 contains additional information specifically related to overcoming fears of driving, and chapter 13 discusses fears of flying. If you fear elevators for reasons unrelated to heights (e.g., feeling like there is not enough air), you should also consider reading chapter 9 on claustrophobia. Remember that people can fear these situations for more than one reason. For example, you might fear driving across bridges because of the possibility of falling off the bridge (because of a height phobia) and because of the possibility of being hit by another driver when the bridge is wet (because of a driving phobia). In such a case, we recommend that you read each chapter that is relevant to your phobia (e.g., chapters 11 and 12).

A Case Example: Height Phobia

■ *Carrie had been at least slightly uncomfortable in high places since childhood. However, her fear gradually increased throughout her teens and twenties. As early as age six, she remembers closing her eyes whenever crossing large bridges. Carrie refused to ski or dive off diving boards higher than two or three feet. Nevertheless, her fear was manageable and didn't really bother her. There were no large bridges where Carrie lived, and most other high places didn't bother her.*

When Carrie was 17, her family vacationed at the Grand Canyon. She was eager to go; however, when they arrived, Carrie couldn't go near the canyon. As she tried to get close to the edge, her heart started to pound. She became short of breath and dizzy, and felt like her legs were about to give out. On the way home, Carrie noticed that elevated areas on the highway bothered her more. She was relieved to finally return home but was disappointed that the trip had been so difficult.

As the years passed, more situations made Carrie feel panicky. When she and her family moved to San Francisco, her bridge phobia became more severe. She found herself driving miles out of her way to avoid bridges and elevated areas. She avoided some parts of the city completely. Interestingly, there was one bridge that Carrie drove over every day to get to work. Although she was frightened the first few times she drove over that bridge, she managed to force herself to do it, and it became easier. However, that didn't seem to make other high places any easier. Carrie avoided going to concerts or plays unless she knew that her seats were not high. Also, she avoided going near the windows when visiting friends in high-rise apartment buildings. Heights seemed to come up several times a week in Carrie's life, and her fear made her life less enjoyable than it might have been if she were comfortable in high places. ■

How Common Are Height Phobias?

About one in five people has a significant fear of heights, and just over 5% of people have a full-blown phobia (Curtis, Magee, Eaton, Wittchen, & Kessler, 1998). This makes height phobias the second-most-prevalent specific phobia (after animal phobias). Unlike many other phobias, which tend to occur much more often in women than in men, height phobias occur as often in men as in women, or may be slightly more common in women. The average age at which height phobias begin is about 15, although they can begin at any age.

Treatment Strategies

In earlier chapters, you began to develop an understanding of your phobia and to plan your treatment. In chapter 3, you identified the specific situations that you fear. You examined whether any of your discomfort was related to the sensations of fear (e.g., feelings that they might lead you to lose control, lose your balance, faint, be embarrassed, have a heart attack). Also, you listed your fearful thoughts regarding the situations you fear and identified some of the obvious and subtle ways that you avoid the situation. Monitoring your fearful reactions will help you plan your treatment and monitor your progress throughout treatment. This chapter will help you improve and refine your previous observations and help you monitor your reactions to high places. We will also provide more-specific instructions on how to change your fearful thoughts, deal with the sensations of fear, prepare for exposure to the feared situation, and carry out the exposure practices.

Step 1: Identifying Specific Fear Triggers

One of the first steps in overcoming any phobia is to identify the specific triggers for your fear. In chapter 3, you identified the particular situations you fear. Below is a list of situations that people with height phobias often fear and avoid. Which of these are frightening to you? Are there any that you would add to the list you developed earlier?

Situations Often Feared and Avoided by People With Height Phobias

- Hiking in high places (e.g., near cliffs, on mountains)

- Visiting tall buildings and looking out the window

- Using escalators, certain elevators, or certain staircases

- Standing near railings (e.g., on balconies)

- Driving or walking over bridges, elevated roads, or ramps

- Pursuing careers involving high places (e.g., construction)

- Standing on chairs or ladders (e.g., to change light bulbs)

- Flying

- Going to theaters or sports stadiums (especially if sitting up high or in the balcony)

- Participating in certain sports (e.g., skiing, diving, parachuting, mountain climbing)

- Going on amusement park rides (e.g., Ferris wheel)

- Using fire escapes

- Fixing the roof

- Climbing trees

- Watching other people be in high places

- Looking up at the sky or the tops of skyscrapers

- Watching films of high places

Of course, height phobias take various forms from person to person. The level of discomfort experienced by a specific person may depend on a variety of factors. Below is a list of variables that can affect a person's fear. Which of these influence how much fear you experience in high places?

Variables That Influence Fear in People With Height Phobias

- Distance from the ground

- Distance from the drop-off

- Presence of movement below

- Whether the situation is open (e.g., does the escalator have high walls?)

- Type of floor (e.g., solid vs. see-through, like a fire escape)

- Movement from behind (e.g., other people walking around)?

- Noise

- Presence of other people (strangers)

- Presence of other people (friends/relatives)

- Duration of exposure

- Slope of the ground

- Holding on to wall or railing vs. not holding on

- Form of presentation (e.g., movies vs. real life)

- Being in a car vs. walking

- Presence of railing or window to prevent falling

- Body position (e.g., sitting vs. standing)

- Presence of wind

- Focus of gaze (e.g., looking out vs. looking straight down)

Step 2: Identifying Fearful Thoughts

In chapter 3, you began to identify some of your unrealistic beliefs about high places. As discussed earlier, these beliefs strongly affect whether you will experience fear upon exposure to heights. For example, if you believe that the railing on a balcony might collapse and that you might fall, it makes sense that you would be more frightened on a balcony than someone who doesn't share this belief. Although many people with height phobias are consciously aware of their fearful predictions, some do not know exactly what they are predicting might happen. Because the fear has existed for so long, a person's fearful thoughts may occur very quickly, automatically, and without awareness. For example, you might be fearful about being on the 30th floor of a tall building even if you're not sure why the situation frightens you. If you are unaware of your fearful thoughts about the situation you fear, exposure practices will help make you aware of thoughts you didn't even realize you had.

Fearful thoughts may include beliefs about the situation, such as (1) high structures such as bridges and railings are not sturdy, (2) I will lose my balance and fall, (3) if there is a noise or movement, I will get distracted and fall, and (4), someone will push me over the edge. However, they may also include beliefs concerning fear that the anxiety itself might lead to something bad happening. For example, you might worry about feeling dizzy and falling, losing control (e.g., being drawn to the edge and jumping), fainting, throwing up, feeling embarrassed, or dying.

Step 3: Identifying Fearful Behaviors and Avoidance Patterns

In chapter 3, you listed some of the ways in which you avoid your feared object or situation, including refusing to encounter high places, escaping, using distraction, using excessive protection, over-relying on safety signals, and using medication, alcohol, or drugs. As discussed earlier, avoidance and escape are effective ways to decrease fear in the short term; however, they contribute to fears and phobias in the long term, meaning that you will become fearful the next time you encounter your phobic object or situation. The reason for this is that avoidance prevents you from learning that what you are most worried about either never or rarely happens, and it prevents you from learning that you can cope with whatever it is you are facing. This learning is critical to the eventual reduction of fears and phobias. To overcome your phobia, it is essential to resist the urge to avoid the situation you fear. The first step in this process is to generate lists of situations you avoid and fearful behaviors you use when exposed to the situation you fear. You began this process in earlier chapters. Now, update your lists if necessary.

Step 4: Revising Your Exposure Hierarchy

In chapter 6 you developed an *exposure hierarchy* (list of feared situations in order of scariness). Now that you have expanded your list of feared situations and the variables that affect your fear intensity, the next step is to expand or revise your exposure hierarchy, if necessary.

Step 5: Finding the Situations Needed for Exposure

Before beginning your exposure practices, take some time to think of places to practice. If seeing high places in movies bothers you, find such films in video. Examples include *Spider Man* and *Mission Impossible 2*. If you rent such a film, remember that you are not watching it for its entertainment value. Rather, you want to find scenes that frighten you because of your phobia. In fact, we recommend that you watch scenes showing heights repeatedly. Rewind the film and watch the difficult scenes until you learn that your feared consequences do not occur or that you can cope, as described in chapters 6 and 7.

For many individuals with height phobias, films of high places are not frightening, and it will be necessary to start with exposure to the real thing. There are many places to find the situations you fear. Ask your friends and relatives for ideas. They may know of places in your neighborhood where you can practice.

If you fear driving over bridges, find out where some of the local bridges are. Find out about their size, tolls, traffic, and other factors that may affect your ability to practice. If balconies bother you, think of friends who live in high-rise apartments that you can visit. Many tall office buildings have large glass windows from which you can look out. Find out where the local glass elevators are. Large hotels often have one.

Phone your local theater or sports stadium. Ask them if you can visit when there is no event taking place to practice being up high. Some places may refuse, but others will say yes. Most people realize that height phobias are very common and will allow you to spend time there if you explain why you want to visit. If you can't visit these places during off-hours, try buying tickets for a play, concert, or sporting event. Make sure to order balcony seats to get maximum benefit from the exposure. The higher, the better. If you can't get seats near the top, get to the show early to spend time near the top. It's very easy to make excuses for not doing the exposure properly. With some imagination, you can usually overcome any obstacles that make it difficult to find high places to practice.

Find out where there are cliffs, mountains, and other areas with large drop-offs where you could hike. These are ideal places for individuals to practice. Find places with railings and without railings. Identify areas with sloped ground and flat ground. The more options for creating different types of practices, the more effective your treatment will be.

Does your neighborhood have any shopping malls with more than one floor? Standing near the railing (and even leaning over it) may be good practice for some people. Borrowing a ladder, if you don't already have one, may also be helpful. Do you know anyone with a rooftop that is easy to access? Do you know anyone with a fire escape? Is there a large parking garage with several levels nearby? What about an amusement park with a Ferris wheel or some other elevated ride? Talk to other people. Together you may think of even more places.

Step 6: Changing Your Thoughts

In chapter 5 you learned to change some of your unrealistic thoughts and predictions about situations involving heights. Several strategies were discussed. First, you were taught to learn everything you can about the situation. This can be done in several ways. If you are afraid that a railing might break when you lean on it, watch others lean on it first. In most cases, you will see that the railing is solid. Ask someone else what it looks like down below, so you won't be surprised. Remember, the more you know about the situation you fear, the more likely you will feel in control and experience less fear.

In chapter 5 you also identified examples of overestimations and catastrophizing. Recall that overestimations refer to when you exaggerate the likelihood that something bad is going to happen. For example, many people with height phobias believe that they are likely to fall. To counter the tendency to overestimate the probability that something bad will occur, examine the evidence. Although it is true that people occasionally fall from high places, the vast majority of people don't fall. If you hear a news report about a bridge collapse, remember to consider the many bridges that remain standing for years. What is the realistic probability that a given bridge will fall when you happen to be on it? By examining the evidence, you will decrease the strength of your unrealistic beliefs and thereby decrease your fear.

Catastrophizing refers to exaggerating how bad some event might be if it were to occur. For example, many believe that the embarrassment of having others notice their fear would be unbearable. It's normal not to want others to notice when we are frightened, but would it really be that bad? What might they think? What would you think of someone who looked nervous in some situation (e.g., public speaking)? Would you think badly of such a person? Probably not.

Ask yourself what would be so bad if what you feared happened, and think about how you could cope. For example, how could you cope with someone noticing that you were fearful? Well, you could explain that you are afraid of heights. Or you could do nothing and let them think what they want. Probably, the worst thing that would happen is you would feel the extreme discomfort that you typically feel from your fear. Even the embarrassment would be manageable.

You can practice changing your thoughts before beginning exposure practices. This will give you courage to do the exposure. If you get the urge to escape during an exposure practice, identifying and challenging your irrational thoughts will help you stay in the situation longer.

Step 7: Beginning Exposure Practices

In chapter 7, you learned how to do exposure practices. You learned that exposure sessions should be prolonged (at least 30 minutes, but ideally even longer), frequent, and predictable. After your practices have become easier, give permission to your helper to introduce some surprises. For example, learn to cope with unexpected movements (e.g., a stick being thrown in front of you) or unexpected loud sounds. Practices should begin with easier items from your hierarchy and gradually progress to more difficult items as each step becomes easier. The rate at which you move to more difficult items is up to you. The faster you try the more difficult steps, the faster you will overcome your fear.

Also, to have long-lasting success, it is important to go beyond what you might want to do. For example, you may have no desire to be able to spend time near high cliffs. However, going beyond what you want to do will have two advantages. First, practicing in very challenging situations will make the smaller steps seem even easier. Second, the more difficult the situations that you master, the less likely your fear will return.

Do not expect the practices to be easy. Typically, individuals feel very uncomfortable during exposure sessions. Crying, screaming, shaking, and panicking are common responses at first. Early in the treatment, you may experience an increase in your anxiety even when you are not in the feared situation. You may also be exhausted after exposure sessions. These feelings are normal and to be expected. They will improve as you continue to work on your fear.

Step 8: Dealing With Your Fear of Sensations

As mentioned in chapter 3, many people experience fear sensations. People often believe that a weak feeling in their legs or a dizzy feeling might lead to falling from a high place. Also, these and other sensations can be misinterpreted as signs that a person will lose control, have a heart attack, embarrass themselves, vomit, or faint. If you are not afraid of the physical sensations associated with your fear, it is not necessary to work on overcoming them, and you can skip this section.

However, if the sensations bother you, there are two main strategies that will likely help. First, use the cognitive strategies discussed in chapter 5. Identify your fearful predictions and examine the evidence for these predictions. For example, if you believe that your dizziness may lead to fainting, examine the evidence. Have you ever fainted in a high place before? Have you ever heard of anyone falling from a high place from feeling faint? What is the realistic probability that this will happen today?

You can counter your catastrophic thoughts about the sensations in a similar way. For example, if you believe people seeing you shake would be awful, try asking yourself, "What would be so awful about it, other than the temporary feeling of embarrassment? How could I deal with the situation if it did happen?" "How might I judge someone if I saw him shake?"

The second strategy for overcoming your fear of sensations is to deliberately bring on these sensations in the situation you fear. After being in the situation becomes easier, use the exercises discussed in chapter 7 to increase the intensity of the sensations you fear while up high. For example, after you become more comfortable walking across a bridge, try crossing the bridge after spinning around a few times to induce the sensations of dizziness. This will help you learn that the sensations are not dangerous. Of course, if you have any medical problems (e.g., heart condition, asthma, epilepsy), remember to check with your doctor before deliberately bringing on the physical symptoms as described in chapter 7.

Homework

✎ Complete the eight steps discussed in this chapter to overcome your phobia.

✎ Review earlier chapters as necessary—especially chapters 3, 5, and 7. Use the forms and tools presented in these earlier chapters to help you use the strategies in this chapter.

Chapter 12   *Driving Phobias*

Is This Chapter Right for You?

This chapter is for you if you answer *yes* to the following:

1. Do I have an unrealistic or excessive fear of driving?

2. Does the fear cause me distress or interfere with my life? For example, Does it bother me that I have this fear? Do I avoid places or activities because of the fear? Is my lifestyle affected by the fear?

3. Am I motivated to get over my fear?

4. Am I willing to tolerate temporary increases in fears and phobias or discomfort to get over my fear?

What Is a Driving Phobia?

A driving phobia is an excessive or unrealistic fear of situations involving driving and typically leads to avoidance of driving. In addition, the fear must cause significant distress or impairment in a person's life before it can be called a phobia. For example, a person who is fearful of driving in large cities but who lives in the country might not be considered to have a phobia. This fear would hardly interfere with the person's life, and it would probably not bother the person to have the fear. For a fear to be called a phobia, it must be excessive or unrealistic and must interfere with an individual's life or cause him or her distress.

Some people with driving phobias avoid driving completely and never obtain their driver's license. Some individuals avoid riding in a car as well. Many people with driving phobias continue to drive, although they may restrict their driving (e.g., drive only short distances, during the day, in good weather). Some people fear driving in heavy traffic (e.g., large cities). Other people find highway driving particularly difficult. For still others, driving at night, in bad weather, or in unfamiliar areas may produce fear.

Specific situations, such as making left turns, merging into traffic, and driving at high speeds, may be difficult as well. Driving phobias tend to affect each person differently.

Despite their efforts to avoid driving, many people with driving phobias continue to drive at least occasionally. However, trips in the car become uncomfortable, particularly when there are surprises on the road (e.g., a truck trying to merge into your lane, the door of a parked car suddenly opening). These encounters usually lead to intense physical discomfort including a rush of arousal or panic (e.g., racing heart, breathlessness, dizziness, shaking, nausea, sweating). In addition, these physical sensations may lead to fears of losing control, fainting, going crazy, being embarrassed, or even dying (e.g., of a heart attack). Many individuals report feeling very tense in the car and may scream or cry. In addition, there is almost always an intense urge to escape from the situation by pulling over or letting someone else drive.

Some people fear driving for reasons unrelated to a driving phobia. For example, people with height phobias often avoid driving on elevated highways, ramps, or bridges for fear of falling off the edge. Someone with claustrophobia (fear of enclosed places) might become fearful in the car because of his or her fear of feeling closed-in. This is typically worse in the backseat of the car, driving through tunnels, and in rush hour traffic that isn't moving. Finally, individuals with agoraphobia often avoid driving for fear of having a panic attack in the car. They tend to be more fearful driving unaccompanied, far from home, on highways and in other places where it is hard to escape, and in heavy traffic. In addition, people with agoraphobia have panic attacks in situations that are unrelated to driving.

Unfortunately, most studies examining the prevalence of driving phobias have not distinguished among the different problems that might lead to a driving phobia. Rather, they have included individuals with other phobias that might lead to avoidance of driving (e.g., height phobia, agoraphobia, claustrophobia). Consequently, there are neither good estimates of the prevalence of driving phobias nor of whether driving phobias are more common in men or women. However, the frequency with which individuals with driving phobias seek help at our centers suggests that the problem is common and probably most common among women.

If you fear driving in high places (e.g., on elevated roads, freeway ramps, bridges) read chapter 11 of this manual as well as this chapter. Chapter 11 contains additional information related specifically to overcoming fears of heights. If you fear driving for reasons related to feeling closed in, read chapter 9 on claustrophobia as well. Remember that driving can be feared for more than one reason. For example, people could fear driving on bridges because they might fall off the bridge and because of the possibility of getting into an accident with another driver (e.g., if the bridge is icy). In such a case, we recommend that you read each chapter that is relevant to your phobia (e.g., chapters 11 and 12).

A Case Example: Driving Phobia

■ *Diane was fearful of driving from the time she first sat behind the wheel of her father's station wagon. She had recently obtained her learner's permit. The first time her father took her to practice driving, the experience was very frightening. Within a few minutes of starting to drive, the car stalled while she was making a left turn at a busy intersection. Several cars were honking and swerving out of the way to avoid hitting her. Diane could feel her heart pounding, and she felt as though she couldn't breathe. She felt paralyzed and didn't know what to do. Her father was very tense and asked to switch seats with Diane. Diane's father drove home and suggested that she learn to drive with a professional instructor instead of with him.*

Diane wondered whether it was worth learning to drive. She lived in a large city and could get around by subway. Also, her boyfriend was happy to drive her around. It was very easy to put off learning to drive. At age 26, Diane finally took driving classes and got her license. However, her husband continued to do most of the driving. Diane walked to work, and drove in her neighborhood only when absolutely necessary. She limited her driving to daylight hours and when the roads were clear. Even being a passenger was difficult for Diane during rush-hour traffic. She feared she would get into an accident and worried about how other drivers would react to her driving. Diane remembered how humiliated she felt when other drivers honked and yelled at her. She was determined to avoid getting into that situation again. Diane managed to live her life around her phobia. She took buses, got rides with friends, and walked whenever possible.

At age 30, Diane was given a big promotion at work that required her to move to a smaller city upstate. She could no longer walk to work. Furthermore, she and her husband now worked in opposite directions from their home. She had no way of getting to her new job. For the first month, she took taxis, but she could not afford to do so indefinitely. It was then that Diane finally decided to seek treatment for her driving phobia. ■

Treatment Strategies

Successful treatment of driving phobias involves a variety of components. These components were discussed in detail in chapters 3 through 7. The remainder of this chapter will discuss specific ways of using these strategies to overcome your driving phobia.

By now, you should have begun to develop an understanding of your phobia and may even have a preliminary treatment plan. In chapter 3, you identified the specific situations you fear. Also, you examined whether any of your discomfort was related to fears and phobias over the sensations of fear (e.g., that a racing heart or dizzy feeling might lead you to lose control, be embarrassed, have a heart attack). You listed your fearful thoughts regarding driving and identified some of the obvious and subtle ways that you avoid driving or riding in a car. Having monitored the situations that trigger your fear and what leads to your fearful thoughts and behaviors, it will be easier to develop a treatment plan and monitor your progress during treatment.

This chapter will help you improve and refine your previous observations and the monitoring of your driving phobia. Also, we will provide more-specific instructions on how to change your fearful thoughts, deal with fears and phobias over the sensations of fear, prepare for exposure practices in the car, and, finally, carry out the exposure practices.

Refining Your Treatment Plan

Step 1: Evaluating and Improving Your Driving Skills

Driving is a skill that needs to be practiced regularly. If you drive frequently, or if your phobia began later in life, you may have adequate driving skills. However, if you have avoided driving for a long time, chances are that your skills may be rusty. If you have had little experience driving, improving your driving skills will be important to overcoming your fear. How are your driving skills? Have you been in several accidents that were your fault? Do you tend to speed, drive too slowly, change lanes without checking to see that it is safe, or follow the car in front of you too closely? Are you able to react quickly to surprises (e.g., being cut off by another car, people opening doors in parked cars, animals or potholes appearing in the road)? Do you drive well in bad weather? Are you able to successfully merge with other traffic when getting on the highway? Are you good at staying in your own lane? Do you know the basic rules of the road (e.g., stopping for school buses, when to yield)? Do you tend to get lost while driving? Can you do simple emergency repairs (e.g., change a tire)? If you are unsure about your skill level, ask someone who drives with you regularly about how skilled he or she thinks you are.

If you need to improve your driving skills, there are several possible approaches. First, consider professional driving classes. Remember, some instructors may be less experienced or skilled at helping people cope with their fear while driving. In fact, we have seen clients who had instructors who were impatient and even rude at times. Explain to the instructor that you fear driving and may require a more patient teaching style than most. If you are not pleased with your instructor, find a new one. Remember, you are the customer and are entitled to have an instructor who is comfortable teaching you despite your fear.

Regardless of whether you take professional lessons, it is important that you practice difficult tasks repeatedly. If changing lanes is hard, spend some time changing lanes. Begin with simpler tasks and move on to more challenging tasks only after mastering the easier situations. For example, if you are trying to learn how to merge with highway traffic, first practice on quiet roads and when there is very little traffic. As your skills improve, begin to practice in more difficult situations. Learning to drive is like learning any other skill (e.g., playing a musical instrument, riding a bicycle). Practice is the only way to improve your driving skills. As your skills improve, your fear will decrease.

The remainder of this chapter will provide additional strategies for overcoming your fear of driving, regardless of your current skill level.

Step 2: Identifying Specific Fear Triggers

One of the first steps in overcoming a driving phobia is identifying the specific triggers for your fear. As described previously, driving phobias are experienced differently by each individual, and the level of fear is greatly affected by numerous variables. Below is a list of factors that often influence fear when driving. Which of these affect your fear?

Variables and Situations Affecting Fear in People With Driving Phobias

- Speed of traffic

- Merging with traffic on the highway (entering the highway)

- Having others merge onto a highway on which you are driving

- Type of car (large vs. subcompact)

- Making left turns

- Changing lanes

- Driving alone versus with passengers (Is driving harder with some passengers than with others?)

- Day of the week (e.g., Saturday nights there may be more intoxicated drivers)

- Weather (rain, snow, or ice vs. clear skies and clear roads)

- Type of road (e.g., busy city street, residential street, highway)

- Driving in unfamiliar areas

- Being a passenger in a car (Is fear worse with some drivers than with others?)

- Amount of traffic (rush hour vs. midday)

- Amount of life stress (e.g., driving after a stressful day at work)

- Surprises (e.g., being cut off by another driver)

- Other drivers following closely behind your car

- Driving in the dark versus driving in daylight

- Driving on elevated areas (e.g., bridges, ramps)

- Driving in construction zones (where roads and lanes are narrower)

- Driving on winding, hilly roads

- Passing pedestrians, cyclists, and parked cars

- Parking the car or backing out of a parking space

- Type of vehicles nearby (e.g., trucks vs. small cars)

- Right lane versus left lane

- Distractions (e.g., playing the radio, talking, using the wiper blades, eating in the car)

Step 3: Identifying Fearful Thoughts

In chapter 3, you began to identify some of your fearful beliefs about driving. As discussed earlier, these beliefs strongly affect whether you will experience fear in the car. For example, if you believe that you will be in a car accident if you drive on the highway, it makes sense that you might avoid highway driving. On the other hand, if you believe that highway driving is relatively safe if you drive carefully, you will less likely be afraid. Most people with driving phobias hold false or exaggerated beliefs about the dangers of driving. As a result, they tend to predict that something negative will happen, when in fact such is unlikely. Although many individuals are consciously aware of these fearful predictions, some are less aware of their thoughts. Because the fear has existed for so long, a person's fearful thoughts may occur very quickly, automatically, and without awareness. If you are unaware of your fearful thoughts about driving, exposure practices will help make you aware of thoughts you didn't even realize you had.

Often, fearful thoughts about driving focus on the possibility of being hit by another car, getting in an accident, or being judged negatively by other drivers. However, other individuals report anxiety over the possibility of something bad happening as a result of the intense physical sensations they feel. For example, some individuals believe that their fears and phobias may lead to fainting, losing control of the car, or even dying.

Step 4: Identifying Fearful Behaviors and Avoidance Patterns

An essential step in overcoming a phobia is changing the subtle and obvious avoidance behaviors that maintain the fear. In chapter 3, you listed some of the ways in which you avoid driving, including refusing to drive, escaping, using distraction, using excessive protection, over-relying on safety signals, and using medication, alcohol, or drugs. In an effort to protect themselves from unexpected dangers when driving, many individuals with driving phobias drive too slowly, stay in a particular lane, and distract themselves with the radio. Other fearful drivers may do the opposite and make sure there are no distracting sounds such as music or chatty passengers. These are all examples of subtle avoidance.

As discussed earlier, avoidance and escape are effective ways to decrease fear in the short term; however, they contribute to fears and phobias in the long term, meaning that you will become fearful the next time you encounter your phobic object or situation. The reason for this is that avoidance prevents you from learning that what you are most worried about either never or rarely happens, and it prevents you from learning that you can cope with whatever it is you are facing. This learning is critical to the eventual reduction of fears and phobias. To overcome your phobia, it is essential to resist the urge to avoid the situation you fear. The first step in this process is to generate lists of situations you avoid and fearful behaviors you use when exposed to the situation you fear. You have began this process in earlier chapters. Now, update your list if necessary.

If you avoid driving completely, it may be difficult to know exactly which subtle avoidance behaviors you would engage in if you were driving. Therefore, this list can be expanded after you begin exposure practices and become more aware of the subtle behaviors you use to avoid or escape from difficult situations involving driving.

Step 5: Revising Your Exposure Hierarchy

In chapter 6 you developed an *exposure hierarchy* (list of feared situations, ordered from easiest to hardest). Now that you have expanded the list of situations you avoid, those that bring on your fear, and the variables that make the fear stronger or weaker, the next step is to update your Exposure Hierarchy, if necessary.

Step 6: Finding the Situations Needed for Exposure

Before beginning your exposure, spend some time listing situations in which you might practice different tasks. For example, if you are fearful of making left turns, make a list of places where you can practice left turns of varying levels of difficulty. If you are fearful of driving on ice, make a list of icy roads and places where you could practice sliding around on the ice safely (e.g., an empty parking lot). If merging with highway traffic is difficult, think of areas of the highway with many exits so you can practice getting on and off the highway repeatedly.

If you don't own a car, it will be necessary to obtain one. You could rent or lease a car. Or you could borrow a car from a friend or relative. If driving with certain types of people (e.g., children, people who are unaware of your phobia) is more difficult, find ways to eventually involve such individuals in your practices. Anticipate obstacles to conducting frequent exposure practices and find ways to overcome them in advance. For example, if you think your best friend won't have time to practice with you frequently enough, think of several friends with whom you can practice.

If you run out of ideas for practices, ask other people for suggestions. If you don't drive much, you may not know of good places to practice. Other people you know can help you come up with ideas. Some situations (e.g., driving in the rain) will be difficult or impossible to create when you want. For these situations, take advantage of them when they do occur (e.g., if you fear driving in the rain, plan to practice the next time it rains).

Step 7: Changing Your Thoughts

In chapter 5 you learned to change some of your unrealistic thoughts and predictions about driving. First, you were asked to learn everything you can about the situation—for example, information about how to drive safely (e.g., the rules of the road) and information about the realistic chances of encountering danger while driving. Even knowing that most car accidents lead to only minor damage and no injuries may help decrease your fear. Make a list of questions that you want answered about driving, and then set out to get answers from reliable sources (e.g., books, the Internet, experienced drivers, mechanics, maps).

In chapter 5 you identified instances when you engage in negative thought patterns such as *probability overestimating* and *catastrophizing*. Recall that an overestimation is when you exaggerate the likelihood that something bad is going to happen. For example, some people who fear driving believe they are more likely to get hit by a drunk driver than is actually the case. Although it is certainly true that some people drive intoxicated and that driving intoxicated is more dangerous than driving sober, you are unlikely to be hit by a drunk driver every time you get into the car. To counter the tendency to overestimate the probability of negative events, examine the evidence. Think of the number of people that you know, and multiply that number by how many times you think each of them has driven in their lives. Now, ask yourself how many times each of them has been hit by a drunk driver. You will discover that the probability of being in an accident on any given trip is much lower than you expected.

Consider another example. You may believe that if you get too nervous, your driving will become so bad that you will drive into another car. To counter this thought, consider the number of times you have felt panicky in the car. Of these times, how many times have your fears and phobias led you to lose control of the car? Again, you should be able to see that the chances of losing control are practically zero. By examining the evidence, you will decrease the strength of your unrealistic beliefs and thereby decrease your fear.

Catastrophizing involves exaggerating how bad an event might be if it did occur. For example, some people who fear driving assume it would be "terrible" if another driver honked at them or judged them to be a poor driver. Individuals who fear the judgments of other drivers may become fearful when there are other cars behind them. Ask yourself "What would be so bad about that? What would happen if another driver got angry and honked at me?", and consider how you could cope if the event actually did occur. How could you handle another driver's becoming impatient? Well, you could ignore the other driver, let the driver pass, drive faster so he or she didn't have to wait, and so on. By considering your options, you will discover that almost any situation is manageable, even though it may be undesirable. Don't stop at the thought, "it would be awful," and don't assume that your beliefs are true. Let yourself think ahead to how you can deal with the situation. Probably the worst thing you will experience is extreme discomfort from your fear. With practice, the discomfort will decrease.

Step 8: Beginning Exposure Practices

Chapter 7 describes how to do exposure practices. Exposure sessions should last anywhere from 30 minutes to several hours. Set aside the time in advance. If you are in a hurry, you will not derive maximum benefit from the session. Plan to stay in the situation long enough to learn that whatever it is you are most worried about never or rarely happens or that you can cope with driving.

Typically, individuals feel very uncomfortable during exposure sessions. Some common initial responses include breathlessness, tension, palpitations, blurred vision, dizziness, and frustration. Early in the treatment, you may experience an increase in negative thoughts about driving. You may even have nightmares. Many clients report being exhausted after practices. Others report increased stress levels, irritability, or a tendency to be startled. These feelings are normal and to be expected; however, they can sometimes lead people to be discouraged and to question whether the treatment is working for them. With repeated exposure, these negative feelings will decrease as your fear subsides.

As described in chapter 7, select easier items from your hierarchy when you first start exposure sessions, and as each step becomes easier, gradually progress to more difficult items. For example, if left turns are difficult, begin practicing at times when there is little traffic. As this gets easier, progress to more difficult intersections. Exposures should be done in a predictable way. For example, you could first practice under conditions that aren't frightening (e.g., as a passenger, with no traffic) so you will have a better understanding of what to expect. Exposure should be structured and done in such a way as to minimize surprises at first. Later, difficult situations can be built into the practices. For example, if having someone drive close behind makes you nervous, you can ask your helper to drive behind you. Making each step in the session predictable and keeping it under your control will make it much easier for your fear to decrease.

Allow yourself to feel any discomfort that arises. Don't fight the feelings, and don't interpret them as meaning that you should stop or space practices further apart. Move through the steps on the hierarchy as quickly as you are willing to. There is no danger in moving too fast. It is OK to skip steps and change your hierarchy as you go along. However, before moving to a more difficult task, you should repeat a step until you learn that your feared consequences do not occur, or that you can cope.

To overcome your fear, you may need between 10 and 20 practice sessions, each lasting between 30 minutes and several hours. Don't worry if you need more sessions for the fear to decrease; you will get there in time. Also, for long-lasting success, it is important to go beyond what you may want to do. For example, you may have no need to drive at rush hour. However, if rush-hour traffic frightens you, we recommend that you practice driving in heavy traffic. Practicing more difficult items will make the smaller steps seem even easier and will make it less likely that the fear will return.

If there are particular aspects of driving that bother you, create the situation to include those aspects. For example, if the thought of annoying another driver bothers you, see if you can get a reaction from other drivers with some harmless behavior. For example, sit at a green light until the driver behind you honks. Although it typically is considered rude to purposely annoy others, doing this a few times will help decrease your fears and phobias over being honked at.

You can change your thoughts before beginning exposure. Changing your negative thoughts will give you courage to do more difficult practices. In addition, challenging your fearful thoughts may help you stay in the situation longer, despite urges to escape.

Step 9: Dealing With Your Fear of Sensations

As mentioned in chapter 3, many people experience fears and phobias over the physical sensations they feel while driving. Specifically, these sensations can lead an individual to feel he or she is about to lose control of the car, have a heart attack, do something embarrassing, or faint. Chapters 5 and 7 discuss in detail how to overcome the fear of these sensations. If you are not afraid of the sensations (e.g., dizziness, racing heart, breathlessness), it will not be necessary to work on overcoming such a fear, and you don't need to spend much time on this section. However, if the sensations bother you, pay close attention to the relevant sections on dealing with your fear of sensations in chapters 5 and 7.

Two main strategies will help you deal with the fear of sensations. First, use the cognitive strategies discussed in chapter 5. Identify the predictions you are making about the physical sensations, and examine the evidence. For example, if you believe that the weak feelings you experience might lead you to faint while driving, examine the evidence. Have you ever fainted while driving? What do you know about fainting and phobias (recall that blood and needle phobias are the only ones typically associated with fainting)? After examining the evidence, do you think your prediction may have been an overestimation?

You can counter your catastrophic thoughts about the sensations in a similar way. For example, what could you do if you have the thought "My heart will race so fast that I won't be able to handle it?" Why do you think you couldn't handle it? What would be so bad about feeling uncomfortable? You are able to handle a racing heart in other situations (e.g., while exercising, having sex, watching scary movies). How can you deal with the racing heart? Would it really be that bad? Remember that your pulse will slow in time, even if you stay in the situation.

The second strategy for overcoming fear of sensations is to deliberately bring on these sensations when in the car (see chapter 7). For example, while driving you could deliberately make your heart pound by holding your breath, or make your arms feel tense by deliberately tensing them. This will help you learn that the sensations are not dangerous. That is, even though your heart is pounding or your muscles are tense, nothing catastrophic happens. Of course, if you have any medical problems (e.g., heart condition, asthma, epilepsy), remember to check with your doctor before doing the symptom-exposure exercises in chapter 7.

Troubleshooting

In chapter 7, we provided possible solutions for some of the most common obstacles that arise during exposure-based treatment. Below, we discuss "problems" that may arise in the context of overcoming driving phobias.

Problem: I don't really avoid driving. I just don't feel comfortable when I drive. It doesn't seem to get any easier.

Solution: Even if you do drive, it is possible that you are not getting the maximum benefit from your exposure. Remember, for exposure to be effective, it is important for it to be frequent, prolonged, and predictable. In addition, it is necessary to eliminate all forms of subtle avoidance (e.g., staying in the "safe" lane, distracting yourself with the radio, only driving on "good" days). Finally, it may be important to spend more time using strategies to change your fearful thoughts and overcome your fear of sensations, if relevant.

Problem: Something unexpected happened while I was driving, and I went into a panic.

Solution: Sometimes there are surprises. Cars will stop unexpectedly. Pedestrians will walk into traffic. People in parked cars will open their doors. You may slide on a slippery road. Notice that when these unexpected things occur, you are still able to cope. It's very important to keep practicing despite your discomfort after an unexpected event. Anticipate these events. Expect the unexpected (as is taught in defensive driving courses). Decide in advance how you will handle such an event. However, no matter how prepared you are, you may still be startled sometimes. That's part of driving. Despite being startled, you will usually be able to stop in time, and your fearful predictions will most likely not come true.

Problem: My fear is too intense for me to drive.

Solution: Use the cognitive countering strategies to identify and change your fearful thoughts. Also, move to a lower item on your hierarchy. For example, if driving at night is too difficult, drive during the day. If highway driving is too difficult during rush hour, drive at a less busy time. Do what you can do. The harder steps will eventually get easier.

Homework

✏ Complete the nine steps discussed in this chapter to overcome your phobia.

✏ Review earlier chapters as necessary—especially chapters 3, 5, and 7. Use the forms and tools presented in these earlier chapters to help you use the strategies discussed in this chapter.

Chapter 13

Flying Phobias

Is This Chapter Right for You?

This chapter is for you if you answer *yes* to the following:

1. Do I have an unrealistic or excessive fear of flying?

2. Does the fear cause me distress or interfere with my life? For example, Does it bother me that I have this fear? Do I avoid places or activities because of the fear? Is my lifestyle affected by the fear?

3. Am I motivated to get over my fear?

4. Am I willing to tolerate temporary increases in fears and phobias or discomfort to get over my fear?

What Is a Flying Phobia?

A flying phobia is an excessive or unrealistic fear of situations involving air travel and typically leads to avoidance of flying. In addition, the fear must cause significant distress or impairment in a person's life before it can be called a phobia. For example, a person with a terrible fear of flying who never has the occasion or desire to fly might not be considered phobic. This fear would probably not interfere with the person's functioning or even bother the individual. Some people with flying phobias avoid flying completely. Others fly when necessary but continue to feel very fearful during the entire flight. Individuals with flying phobias who continue to fly tend to use more subtle avoidance strategies during the flight, including distraction (e.g., music, reading), taking medication, drinking alcohol, and flying only under certain conditions (e.g., on particular types of planes, during certain seasons).

Most people with flying phobias report anxiety about the possibility that the airplane will crash or be hijacked. A variety of factors may influence the degree of fear experienced by any particular individual. Often, bad weather, turbulence, and unusual noises on the airplane heighten fear. Similarly, the length of the flight, and certain parts of the flight (e.g., takeoffs, landings) may influence an individual's fear level. Even being at the airport or thinking about entering an airplane might lead to extreme fear for some people.

Despite their efforts to avoid flying, many people with flying phobias continue to fly occasionally. However, airplane trips remain uncomfortable, particularly when there are surprises (e.g., delays, turbulence). These trips usually lead to intense physical discomfort, including a rush of arousal or panic (e.g., racing heart, breathlessness, dizziness, shaking, nausea, sweating). These physical sensations may lead to fears of losing control, vomiting, fainting, going crazy, being embarrassed, or even dying (e.g., of a heart attack). In addition, individuals with flying phobias almost always experience an intense urge to escape from the situation, which in and of itself may become a source of further fear (i.e., the image of trying to get out of a plane in mid-flight).

Some people avoid flying for reasons unrelated to a specific flying phobia. For example, people with height phobias often avoid flying because they fear being up high. Takeoffs or landings do not especially frighten them: their fear is worse when the plane is high in the air because of their fear of being far from the ground. Window seats might be especially difficult because they can see how high the plane is off the ground. Someone with claustrophobia (fear of enclosed places) might become fearful about feeling closed-in on an airplane. This reaction typically is worse in small or crowded planes. The person with claustrophobia probably prefers to sit by the window to have an open view, or by the aisle to have more room to move around if necessary. The restroom on the airplane might be especially frightening because it is small. Finally, people with agoraphobia (a fear of places from which escape might be difficult in the event of a panic attack) often avoid flying. Like claustrophobia, agoraphobia is typically associated with a fear of being trapped, as opposed to a fear of crashing.

If you fear flying because you fear heights, read chapter 11 of this manual; it contains additional information specifically related to overcoming fears of heights. If you fear flying for reasons related to feeling closed-in, read chapter 9 on claustrophobia. However, remember that people can fear and avoid flying for more than one reason. Someone might avoid flying because of a fear of crashing (flying phobia) and a fear of being closed-in (claustrophobia). In such a case, we recommend that you read each chapter that is relevant to your phobia (e.g., chapters 9 and 13).

How Common Are Flying Phobias?

About 13% of the population has an extreme fear of flying, and about 3.5% of people fear flying to the point of having a full-blown specific phobia (Curtis et al., 1998). Fears of flying and related situations appear to be more prevalent in women than in men (Bourdon et al., 1988). On average, the fear begins in one's twenties, which is considerably older than for some types of phobia (e.g., animal phobias) but similar to the age of onset for others (e.g., claustrophobia).

A Case Example: Flying Phobia

■ *It seemed like every time Julia opened the newspaper or turned on the television, there was another news story about a plane crash that had killed hundreds of passengers. Julia had not been comfortable traveling by air since a very turbulent flight at age 19, though for years she flew anyway, particularly short flights on large planes.*

More recently, Julia's fear increased dramatically. Each time she flew, she felt sure her plane would crash. She wondered, "If flying is so safe, why do they spend so much time warning passengers about what to do in case of an emergency?" Every time a plane crash was reported in the media, she experienced an increase in apprehension over flying. Julia had decided that she would never fly again and felt fine about her decision.

Several years passed, and Julia was working as an architect in New York City. Her family typically visited her from the West Coast once a year. However, her father was experiencing health problems and could no longer travel. Julia hadn't seen her family in more than three years. She began to feel very guilty about not seeing them, especially since her father had become ill. In addition, her husband had been urging her to take a vacation with him. He was tired of traveling by car and wanted to spend a few weeks with Julia overseas. Despite these pressures, Julia found excuses not to travel and continued to avoid airplanes.

Julia finally managed to fly home to see her family once. She had five drinks on the trip and found that alcohol made her feel significantly better while flying. However, she knew that drinking wasn't the answer to her problem and decided to seek help for her phobia. It wasn't until two years later that she fi-

nally sought treatment, under much pressure from her husband, who had become very distressed about not being able to travel. ■

Treatment Strategies

In earlier chapters, you began to develop an understanding of your phobia and may even have a preliminary treatment plan. In chapter 3, you identified the specific situations that you fear. You also examined whether any of your discomfort was related to fears and phobias over the sensations of fear (e.g., that they may lead you to lose control, be embarrassed, have a heart attack). You listed your fearful thoughts about flying and identified some of the obvious and subtle ways that you avoid doing so. Having monitored the situations that trigger your fear and your fearful thoughts and behaviors, it will be easier to develop a treatment plan and monitor your progress during treatment.

This chapter will help you expand and clarify your previous observations and the monitoring of your flying phobia. In addition, you will receive more-specific instructions on how to change your fearful thoughts, deal with fears and phobias over the sensations of fear, prepare for exposure practices, and, finally, carry out the exposure practices.

Refining Your Treatment Plan

Step 1: Identifying Specific Fear Triggers

One of the first steps in overcoming a flying phobia is to identify the specific triggers for your fear. Flying phobias are experienced differently by each individual, and the level of fear is greatly affected by numerous factors. Below is a list of situations and variables that can affect fear in people with flying phobias. Which of these are relevant for you?

Variables and Situations Affecting Fear in People With Flying Phobias

■ Size of airplane

■ Sounds on the airplane

- Number of passengers, crowdedness of airplane

- Whether flight is delayed, reason for delay

- Bad weather (e.g., rain, fog)

- Time of day (light vs. dark)

- Seating (aisle, window, etc.)

- Listening to the safety information before taking off

- Turbulence

- Snow or ice on the ground

- Surface down below (e.g., water, mountains, flat land)

- Taking off

- Landing

- Duration of flight

- Altitude of airplane (e.g., above or below clouds)

- Presence of friend or relative

- Amount of life stress (e.g., flying after a stressful day at work)

- Commercial versus privately owned airplanes

- Size of airport

Step 2: Identifying Fearful Thoughts

In chapter 3, you began to identify some of your fearful beliefs about flying. As discussed earlier, these beliefs strongly affect whether you will experience fear in an airplane. For example, it makes sense that you might avoid flying if you believe your plane will crash. On the other hand, you would be less afraid if you believed flying were a perfectly safe method of travel. Most people with flying phobias hold false or exaggerated beliefs about the safety of air travel. As a result, they predict that they are in danger, when in fact the situation is very safe. Although many individuals are consciously aware of these fearful predictions, some do not know exactly what they are predicting might happen. Because the fear has existed for so long, a person's fearful thoughts may occur very quickly, automatically, and without awareness. If you are unaware of your fearful thoughts about flying, exposure practices will help you become aware of your thoughts.

Often, fearful thoughts about flying are focused on the possibility of harm from being in the situation. Examples of such fearful thoughts include: (1) the airplane will crash, (2) I will be injured, (3) the pilot is not competent, (4) the pilot has been drinking, (5) the plane will have mechanical problems, (6) my flight will be delayed, (7) my luggage will get lost, (8) the pilot will not be able to maneuver the plane in bad weather, (9) the noises I hear indicate a serious problem, and (10) the plane will be hijacked or bombed. Many individuals also report fears and phobias about possible danger from the intense anxiety and physical sensations they feel (e.g., dizziness, racing heart). For example, some individuals believe that their sensations of fears may lead to fainting, vomiting, losing control, or running up and down the aisle screaming.

Step 3: Identifying Fearful Behaviors and Avoidance Patterns

An essential step in overcoming a phobia is changing the behavior patterns that maintain the fear. Types of subtle and obvious avoidance were discussed in previous chapters. In chapter 3, you listed some of the ways in which you avoid flying, including refusing to fly, escaping, using distraction, using excessive protection, over-relying on safety signals, and using medication, alcohol, or drugs. In an effort to protect themselves from unexpected dangers when flying, many individuals with phobias of air travel drink alcohol or use anti-anxiety medications on the airplane. They may request certain "safe" seats or distract themselves with music, conversation, or a book. Others may fly only on certain types of aircraft, at certain times of day, or with certain individuals (e.g., close friends or family members).

As discussed earlier, avoidance and escape are effective ways to decrease fear in the short term; however, they contribute to fears and phobias in the long term, meaning that you will become fearful the next time you encounter your phobic object or situation. The reason for this is that avoidance prevents you from learning that what you are most worried about either never or rarely happens, and it prevents you from learning that you can cope with whatever it is you are facing. This learning is critical to the eventual reduction of fears and phobias. To overcome your phobia, it will be essential to resist the urge to avoid the situation you fear. The first step in this process is to generate lists of situations you avoid and fearful behaviors you use when exposed to the situation you fear. You began this process in earlier chapters. Now, update your list if necessary.

If you avoid air travel completely, it may be difficult to know exactly which behaviors you engage in. Therefore, this list can be expanded after you begin exposure practices and become more aware of the subtle behaviors you use to avoid or escape from difficult situations involving air travel.

Step 4: Revising Your Exposure Hierarchy

In chapter 6 you developed an *exposure hierarchy* (list of feared situations, ordered from easiest to hardest). Now that you have expanded the list of situations you avoid, those that bring on your fear, and the variables that weaken or strengthen the fear, the next step is to update or revise your exposure hierarchy, if necessary.

Step 5: Finding the Situations Needed for Exposure

Compared to getting over other phobias, overcoming a fear of flying is relatively expensive because of the cost of taking commercial flights. At some point it will be necessary to take a plane to overcome your fear. However, there are many smaller steps before that, and they cost very little. For example, if just being at the airport is fear provoking, you should practice being there for extended periods. Do the activities that might make you fearful if you were taking a real flight (e.g., standing in the ticket line, waiting at the gate, watching the planes take off). Consider trying to get permission to sit on an airplane. Although airlines at commercial airports will not allow you to do this, private pilots or flight schools may permit you to sit on an aircraft at no charge.

Certain amusement park rides simulate some of the sensations of flying. If you have such a park or fair nearby, check to see if there are any rides that might frighten you because they feel similar to flying in an airplane. In addition, there is now virtual reality (VR) computer software available that will simulate the experience of being on an airplane. You can check to see whether a therapist in your area offers VR treatments for flying phobia. One company (Virtually Better, Inc.) that produces such software for professionals has a list of VR therapists on their web site (http://www.virtuallybetter.com).

Imaginal exposure is another method of practicing exposure without actually flying. Imaginal exposure involves imagining that you are in a frightening situation. The goal of imaginal exposure is to visualize being in the situation vividly enough to experience an increase in your fear level. To do this effectively, imagine experiencing the situation with all your senses. In other words, picture what the airplane might look like inside, including the passengers and flight crew, the seats, your bag under the seat in front of you, the lights, and so on. Also, be aware of the smells, sounds, and sensations that you might experience on an airplane. Imagine your heart pounding, your ears "popping," your stomach feeling queasy, the air blowing, and any other sensations you feel when you are flying. The more realistic your image, the more fear you will feel initially. However, with repeated practice, your fear of flying will gradually decrease. If your fear and anxiety is high during imaginal exposure practices, that is a sign that you are doing the exercises properly. Imaginal exposure is difficult and takes much practice to use effectively. If you have problems becoming fearful while using imaginal exposure, don't give up. Keep practicing until it becomes easier, or try to use some of the other methods mentioned in this chapter.

At some point it will be necessary to practice flying on a real airplane. Call airlines that serve your local airport to find out what the least expensive routes are. If you are fearful of takeoffs and landings, practice flying on routes with multiple stopovers. If you are fearful of being in the air, practice on longer flights. If smaller airplanes frighten you, arrange to fly in and out of smaller airports, which often use smaller aircraft. Private pilots and small airlines may be able to fly you on smaller planes and at a reduced cost. There may be pilots available who will take passengers for short flights over your city at relatively low fares. Flights such as these would save you the expense and inconvenience of having to fly to another place. Staff at your local airport or flight schools may be aware of private companies or pilots who offer this service. Check your local business directory. If you are using a private airplane, mention to the pilot that you have a fear of flying and ask that the ride be as smooth as possible.

Some individuals overcome their flying phobia by taking flying lessons. This may seem like an extreme method of getting over one's fear, but it works. If you think you might be interested in taking flying classes, check your telephone directory under "aircraft schools."

Finally, some companies offer programs for overcoming flying phobias. In the past, many airlines in North America offered such programs, but most seem to have been discontinued in recent years. Many of the current programs are run by flight specialists (e.g., airline captains), mental health professionals (e.g., psychologists), or both. They focus on providing facts and information on the mechanical features of airplanes and their safety features. Often, they also provide strategies for managing your fears and phobias (e.g., doing relaxation exercises, taking tours of airline hangars, and even flying on a commercial airline). Some examples of programs you may want to check out are listed below, along with their web sites (though note that we do not have any firsthand experience with these programs and therefore are not recommending any particular program from this list):

- Aviatours (British Airways): http://www.aviatours.co.uk (UK only)

- Calm Flight: http://www.calmflight.com (Westchester County, NY)

- Fear of Flying Clinic: http://www.fofc.com (San Mateo, CA)

- Fearless Flight: http://www.fearless-flight.com (courses in Phoenix, AZ, or over the Internet)

- Fearless Flying: http://www.fearlessflying.com (a mail-order program)

- My Sky: http://www.myskyprogram.com (weekend program in Eagan, MN)

- SOAR: http://www.fearofflying.com (a video course on 10 DVDs)

- Virgin Atlantic Airlines: http://www.flyingwithoutfear.info (UK only)

If you have trouble thinking of inexpensive ways to practice, ask other people for suggestions. They might be able to come up with ideas. For example, you may have a friend who knows of a service that offers short airplane rides. You may even have a friend who has a pilot's license or knows someone else who flies. Your helper and other people you know can assist you in coming up with ideas. For every situation that bothers you, you should try to come up with ways of creating that situation. Two web sites that include additional resources for flying phobias are http://www.airafraid.com and http://www.airsafe.com/issues/fear.htm.

Step 6: Changing Your Thoughts

In chapter 5 you learned to change some of your unrealistic thoughts and predictions about air travel. Several strategies were discussed. First, you were asked to learn everything that you can about flying and airline safety. Information can be found in several places. A good place to start is on the Internet or at your local library or bookstore. Books on air travel and on flying phobias may be helpful for generating relevant information. For example, most individuals who fear flying are not aware of the fact that according to the National Transportation Safety Board, only 104 Americans died each year in the 1980s from a commercial airline accident. Compare that to the 8,000 people who died each year from accidents related to being a pedestrian (e.g., walking across the street) and you will see that flying is relatively safe. In fact, the chances of dying in an airline accident have been estimated to be about 1 in 10 million. It may seem higher to you because every time a plane crashes, the story is all over the news for several days, whereas more common ways of accidentally dying (e.g., falling, car accidents) hardly ever make it to the news. Actually, the fact that plane crashes are so newsworthy should be taken as a sign that they are relatively infrequent. You may hear about a commercial airline crash every year or two, but remember, many thousands of flights take off and land safely each day.

In addition to finding safety statistics, you may want to seek out information on the training and experience of airline pilots, how an airplane stays in the air, airplane maintenance, the air traffic control system, weather, and turbulence. You can also find detailed information about commercial airline flights, including airplane inspection, servicing and maintenance, closing doors, various noises (e.g., chimes, engines, air conditioning, brake noises, hydraulic pump activation, landing gear), various sights (e.g., flight crew moving around, lights flickering), and various sensations (e.g., vibrations, changes in air pressure, acceleration, changes in altitude, changes in speed). Learning about the normal sights, sounds, and sensations you can expect on a plane will help decrease your fears and phobias when experience them. In the recommended readings section at the end of this book, we list books that contain such information.

As well as learning about the flying experience from books, ask your friends about their experiences of flying. Find out what is normal and what you should expect during a commercial flight. The more you know in advance, the less distressing the flight will be. Make a list of questions you want answered about flying and then set out to get answers from reliable sources (e.g., books, friends, flight crew members).

In chapter 5 you identified instances when you have engaged in negative thought patterns such as *probability overestimating* and *catastrophizing*. Recall that an overestimation is when you exaggerate the likelihood of something bad happening. For example, many people who fear flying incorrectly believe that their plane is likely to crash. Although it is true that airplanes occasionally crash, the vast majority of flights arrive safely. To counter the tendency to overestimate the probability of negative events, examine the evidence. Think of the number of people you know, then multiply that number by how many times you think each of them has flown in their lives. Add in all the people who you don't know who fly. When you are at the airport, pay attention to how many flights take off in an hour. Multiply that by 15 hours (assuming your flight occurs during the hours of 6 A.M. and 9 P.M.) to estimate the number of flights in a day. Multiply that by the number of days in a year and the number of airports in the country to get an idea of the number of commercial flights each year in the United States. Now, ask yourself how many times you have read about a plane crashing in the past year. When you take into account all the flights that arrive safely, chances are you will discover that the probability of being in a plane crash is practically zero.

Consider another example. You may believe that if you get too nervous, you may stop breathing or your heart may pound so much that you will have a heart attack or lose control. To counter this thought, consider the number of times you have felt panicky before. Of these times, on how many occasions have your fears and phobias led you to lose control or have a heart attack? Again, you should be able to see that the realistic chances of these things occurring are practically zero. By examining the evidence, you will decrease the strength of your unrealistic beliefs and thereby decrease your fear.

Catastrophizing is when you exaggerate how bad an event might be if it did occur. For example, some people who fear flying assume it would be "terrible" if the person next to them noticed that they were nervous. Other people might think it would be unmanageable if they vomited on a commercial flight. Ask yourself "What would be so bad about that? What would happen if another passenger did notice my shaking? What if I did have to use the air sickness bag?" and consider how you could cope if the event actually did occur. How might you handle another passenger's staring at you if you got shaky? Well, you could ignore the other person, explain that you were nervous, explain that you didn't get enough sleep the night before, tell him or her to stop looking at you, and so on. By considering different ways of coping, you will discover that almost any situation is manageable, even though it may be uncomfortable.

Don't stop at the thought, "it would be awful," and don't assume that your beliefs are true. Let yourself think ahead to how you can deal with the situation. Probably the worst thing you will experience is extreme discomfort. With practice, the discomfort will decrease.

Step 7: Beginning Exposure Practices

Chapter 7 describes how to do exposure practices. Exposure sessions should last anywhere from 30 minutes to several hours, although the exact duration will depend on the specific flight on which you practice. Set aside the time in advance. If you are in a hurry, you will not derive maximum benefit from the session. Remember, the goal is to learn that whatever it is you are most worried about rarely or never happens and that you can cope with flying.

These sessions will not be easy. Typically, individuals feel very uncomfortable during the exposure sessions. Some common initial responses include breathlessness, tension, palpitations, blurred vision, dizziness, and frustration. Early in the treatment, you are likely to experience an increase in negative thoughts about flying. You may even have nightmares. Many individuals report being exhausted after exposure sessions. Others report an increase in overall stress levels, irritability, and a tendency to be startled. These feelings are normal and are to be expected; however, they can sometimes lead people to be discouraged and to question whether the treatment is working for them. Don't give up. Repeated exposure will lead to a reduction in your fear and in these other unpleasant experiences.

As described in chapter 7, select easier items from your hierarchy when first starting exposure sessions, and as each step becomes easier, gradually progress to more difficult items. For example, if small planes are especially difficult, begin with larger planes and progress to smaller aircraft as travel on larger planes gets easier.

Allow yourself to feel any discomfort that arises. Don't fight the feelings, and don't interpret them as meaning that you should stop or slow down.

You should move through the steps on the hierarchy as quickly as you are willing to. There is no danger in moving too fast. It is OK to skip steps and change your hierarchy as you go. However, before moving to a more difficult task, you should repeat the easier practice until you learn that your feared consequences do not occur, or that you can cope.

To overcome your fear, you may need 5 or 10 practice flights, although, in many cases, people with flying phobias are able to overcome their fear in fewer flights. Don't worry if you need more sessions for the fear to decrease; you will get there in time. In addition, to have long-lasting success, it is important to go beyond what you may want to do (e.g., fly more frequently, in a variety of planes). Also, practicing more difficult items will make the smaller steps seem even easier and will make it more likely that the fear won't return.

Changing your negative thoughts will help give you the courage to do more difficult practices. In addition, identifying and challenging your irrational thoughts may help you stay in the exposure situation longer without turning to subtle types of avoidance or escape (e.g., alcohol, distraction).

Step 8: Dealing With Your Fear of Sensations

As mentioned in chapter 3, many people experience fears and phobias over the physical sensations they feel while flying. Specifically, these sensations can make an individual feel like they are about to lose control, have a heart attack, embarrass themselves, vomit, or faint. Chapters 5 and 7 discuss in detail how to overcome the fear of these sensations. If you are not afraid of the sensations (e.g., dizziness, racing heart, breathlessness), it will not be necessary to work on overcoming such a fear, and you don't need to spend much time on this section. However, if the sensations bother you, pay close attention to the relevant strategies in chapters 5 and 7.

Two main strategies will help you deal with the fear of sensations. First, use the cognitive strategies discussed in chapter 5. Identify the predictions you are making about the fear sensations, and examine the evidence. For example, if you believe that your fear will get so intense that you might run to the door and try to open it, examine the evidence. Have you ever lost control while flying? Have you ever heard of an individual opening the airplane door because of their fear? After examining the evidence, do you think your prediction may have been an overestimation?

You can counter your catastrophic thoughts about the sensations in a similar way. For example, what could you do if you have the thought "My heart will race so fast that I won't be able to handle it?" Why do you think you couldn't handle it? What would be so bad about feeling uncomfortable? You are able to handle a racing heart in other situations (e.g., when exercising, having sex, watching scary movies). How could you deal with the racing heart? Would it really be that bad? Remember, your pulse will slow in time, even if you stay in the situation.

The second strategy for overcoming your fear of sensations is to deliberately bring on these sensations when in the feared situation (see chapter 7). For example, you could deliberately make your heart pound by taking a few deep breaths and hyperventilating while on the airplane. Or you could hold your breath to induce breathlessness. Or you could resist the urge to use the cool air stream, and force yourself to remain hot. Exercises such as these will help you learn that the sensations are not dangerous. Of course, if you have any medical problems (e.g., heart condition, asthma, epilepsy), remember to check with your doctor before doing the symptom-exposure exercises described in chapter 7.

Troubleshooting

In chapter 7, we provided possible solutions for some of the most common obstacles that arise during exposure-based treatment. Below, we discuss additional "problems" that may arise in the context of overcoming flying phobias.

Problem: I don't really avoid flying. I just don't feel comfortable when I fly. It doesn't seem to get any easier.

Solution: Even if you do fly, it is possible that you are not getting the maximum benefit from your exposure. Remember, for exposure to be effective, it is important for it to be frequent, prolonged, and predictable. In addition, it is necessary to eliminate all forms of subtle avoidance (e.g., distraction, alcohol, music). Subtle avoidance strategies will decrease your fear and anxiety temporarily, but your fear will increase again when your attention returns to your flight. Distraction will lead to your fear going up and down for the entire flight rather than increasing initially and gradually decreasing over time. Finally, if you find that your fear remains high, it may be important to spend more time using strategies to change your fearful thoughts and overcome your fear of sensations, if relevant.

Problem: Something unexpected happened while I was flying (e.g., turbulence), and I went into a panic.

Solution: Sometimes there are surprises. Notice that when these unexpected things occur, you still are able to cope. It's very important to keep practicing despite the discomfort following an unexpected event. Anticipate these events. Decide in advance how you will handle them. However, no matter how prepared you are, you may still be startled sometimes. Despite being startled, your fearful predictions will most likely not come true.

Homework

✎ Complete the eight steps discussed in this chapter to overcome your phobia.

✎ Review earlier chapters as necessary—especially chapters 3, 5, and 7. Use the forms and tools presented in these earlier chapters to help you use the strategies discussed in this chapter.

Chapter 14

Phobias of Storms, Water, Choking, and Vomiting

Is This Chapter Right for You?

This chapter provides information on overcoming the following specific phobias: storms, choking, vomiting, and water. In addition to reading this chapter, it is essential that you read chapters 1 through 7 very carefully. This chapter discusses additional ideas to supplement those provided in the first part of this manual, but it assumes that you already have a good understanding of the basic principles discussed in the first parts of this book.

As with the specific phobias discussed in previous chapters, successful treatment for the phobias discussed in this chapter will involve the components discussed in detail in chapters 3 through 7. By now, you should have begun to develop an understanding of your phobia and to craft a preliminary treatment plan. In chapter 3, you began to identify the specific situations that you fear. In addition, you examined whether any of your discomfort was related to fears and phobias over the sensations of fear (e.g., that they might lead you to lose control, be embarrassed, have a heart attack). You listed your fearful thoughts and identified some of the obvious and subtle ways that you avoid the situation. Having monitored the situations that trigger your fear and noted your fearful thoughts and behaviors, it will be easier to develop a treatment plan and monitor your progress during treatment.

The remainder of this chapter will help you improve and refine your previous observations, self-monitoring, and treatment plan for your specific phobia if you fear one or more of the situations discussed in this chapter. It will not be necessary to read this entire chapter. You need read only the parts relevant to the specific situations you fear (i.e., storms, choking or vomiting, water).

Storm Phobias

Storm phobias are relatively common. About 1 in 11 people in the general population has an extreme fear of storms, and about 3% of people fear storms at a level that would be considered a phobia (Curtis, Magee, Eaton, Wittchen,

& Kessler, 1998). Storm phobias are about three times more common in women than in men (Bourdon et al., 1988). Many people who fear storms are especially fearful during thunderstorms, although individuals often report fears and phobias over other types of storms, including severe windstorms (e.g., hurricanes, tornados), heavy rainstorms, and winter storms.

Overview of Treatment

The process of overcoming a fear of storms involves three main components. The first step is *preparation*. Preparing to overcome your fear involves identifying the most important aspects of the problem, including the situations that trigger your fear, the variables that affect the intensity of your fear in these situations, the behaviors you use to protect yourself when feeling fearful, and the beliefs that contribute to your fear. The second component of treatment involves using the *cognitive strategies* discussed in chapter 6 to challenge your unrealistic, fearful predictions and to replace them with more realistic thoughts. The third, and perhaps most important, component is *exposure* to the feared situation. Exposure involves confronting situations that frighten you, but it also involves stopping some of the unnecessary safety behaviors you currently use to protect yourself from possible danger, particularly when the true risk is minimal.

Identifying Triggers, Behaviors, and Thoughts

Before you can begin to overcome your fear of storms, it is important to understand the triggers for your fear, your behavior when frightened, and the thoughts and beliefs associated with your fear. Phobias are experienced differently by each individual, and the level of fear is greatly affected by numerous variables. Examples of factors that often affect levels of fear in people with storm phobias include:

- Presence and amount of thunder or other noise

- Lightning

- Intensity of wind, rain, or hail

- Duration of storm

- Being alone versus being accompanied

- Location (e.g., living room, car, outside, basement, bathroom)

- Darkness of sky

- Time of day

- Window in the room

- Whether there has been an official storm warning

Are any of these relevant to your fear? What are some of the factors that make your fears and phobias stronger or weaker with respect to storms?

Next, note the specific behaviors in which you engage because of your fear of storms. For example, do you avoid certain activities (e.g., being far from home) on days when bad weather is expected? Do you restrict yourself to certain rooms (e.g., basement, bathroom, rooms with no windows) and perform certain activities (close eyes, listen to music, remain near people) during storms? Do you frequently check weather reports to make sure that no storms are expected? In chapter 3, you learned about ways in which people avoid the situations they fear, including refusing to enter the situation, escaping, using distraction, using excessive protection, over-relying on safety signals, and using medication, alcohol, or drugs. Make sure you have a complete list of all the situations and activities you avoid during storms or when you expect a storm to occur. Also, make a list of behaviors you use to protect yourself from "danger" during a storm. These lists will help you identify the types of behaviors to change as you overcome your phobia.

Finally, identify the types of fearful predictions you make during storms. For example, some individuals fear the possibility of property damage during a storm. Others believe they are likely to be killed or injured during a storm (e.g., by being struck by lightning). Some people also fear the sensations that they experience during storms. For example, a racing heart might be interpreted as a sign of an impending heart attack. Other sensations might be interpreted as leading one to lose control, go crazy, faint, or do something embarrassing. What types of fearful predictions do you make regarding storms and the negative things that might happen during a storm?

Changing Fearful Thoughts

Strategies for changing overestimations and catastrophic thoughts were discussed in detail in chapter 5. This process involves examining the evidence for your fearful predictions and considering ways in which you could cope with storms (e.g., "If I wait out a storm, it will eventually pass, just like it has in the past"), rather than focusing on how terrible a storm would be if it were to occur (e.g., "I don't think I could manage if there were a storm today"). We will not review these strategies here, so we recommend that you read chapter 5 again if necessary.

In addition to challenging overestimations and catastrophic thinking, it is important to learn whatever you can about storms to replace any misinformation you may be carrying around in your head with more accurate and unbiased information. For example, if you are fearful of being struck by lightning, read as much as you can about lightning and thunderstorms. Don't focus just on the negative information (e.g., newspaper articles about people dying in storms). To make a realistic appraisal of the dangers involved in a thunderstorm, pay attention to all relevant information (including all the people who don't get struck by lightning).

For example, according to a 1994 article in *Omni* magazine about thunderstorms, at any given moment, there are 2,000 thunderstorms occurring on the planet. Each storm generates a flash of lightning every 20 seconds. In other words, lightning strikes about 100 times per second. Given the frequency of lightning strikes, you might expect many individuals to be injured; however, this is simply not the case. According to recent statistics, only 1 person in 1.9 million dies from being struck by lightning. Similarly, only 1 in 450,000 Americans will die in a tornado. Compare these figures to the chances of dying from a smoking-related illness (1 in 600 people will die of a smoking-related illness before the age of 35), and you will see that it is unusual to die in storm-related accidents.

We are not saying that nobody ever dies from damage caused by storms. In fact, storms like Hurricane Katrina, which destroyed much of New Orleans in 2005, cause serious damage each year. In certain geographical regions, possible danger from flooding, landslides, icy roads, and strong winds are a realistic concern. In regions where the risks are real, residents should be careful to take reasonable precautions and to ensure that they have adequate insurance.

However, for typical storms, damage is minimal, especially when minimal precautions are taken (e.g., driving more slowly). The fact that deaths from bad storms are reported in the news media should be taken as evidence that such deaths are unusual. The news does not typically report deaths from everyday causes. Your newspaper may report a story of a local person being struck by lightning, but when is the last time you read about a local person dying from a heart attack? Unusual events, not ordinary ones, tend to make it the news.

We suggest that you make a list of questions you have about storms and set out to find answers at the library, a local bookstore, or on the Internet. The more you know about storms, the less frightening they will be. Be sure to use reliable sources. For example, information on a web site designed to raise funds for hurricane relief may be biased in favor of discussing unusually devastating storms, compared to a web site designed to provide education about the nature of thunder and lightning.

Confronting Feared Situations Through Exposure

Unfortunately, we cannot create a storm whenever and wherever we might need one, which makes it difficult to schedule exposure practices. In some parts of the United States, storms are sometimes predictable. For example, Arizona has a monsoon season in the summer, during which there are severe afternoon thunderstorms. However, in most parts of the country you won't be able to arrange exposure practices in advance. You will need to be flexible and prepared to use the necessary strategies when a storm occurs.

There are some things that you can do to prepare for exposure to real storms. Repeated *imaginal exposure* to storms may help decrease your fear when an actual storm occurs. Imaginal exposure is a method of practicing exposure without actually being in the feared situation. Imaginal exposure involves closing your eyes and imagining that you are in a frightening situation. The goal of imaginal exposure is to picture being in the situation vividly enough to experience an increase in your anxiety level. To do this effectively, imagine experiencing the situation with all your senses. In other words, picture what the situation might look like, including all the associated details. Also, be aware of the smells, sounds, and sensations you might experience if you were in the feared situation. The more realistic your image, the more fear that you will feel and the more your fear will eventually decrease with repeated practice.

As a first step in learning to do imaginal exposure, it is a good idea to start with a neutral or nonfearful image. For example, close your eyes and imagine sitting in an empty room with four walls and an open window. Be aware of the size of the room and the color of the walls. For the purpose of this exercise, imagine that all four walls are painted blue. Imagine the temperature of the room to be comfortable, and let yourself feel a soft breeze coming in through the window. Be aware of the smell of the flowers coming in with the breeze. Hear the sounds of the birds outside the window. Imagine the scene with all your senses.

With practice, you will become better at imagining the neutral scene described above. When you can picture a vivid image of the blue room, imagine being in your feared situation. Use all the same strategies described for the blue room, but change the details of your image to match the situation that you fear. For example, imagine sitting near an open window with a severe thunderstorm outside. Imagine the light from the lightning and the sound of the thunder. Also, imagine feeling any physical sensations that you typically experience during storms (e.g., muscle tension, racing heart).

To enhance the imaginal exposure experience, we recommend that you consider listening to a recording of thunderstorms, rain, wind, or any other sounds that frighten you during storms. Such recordings are often available in music stores, nature stores, and on the Internet. If you sit in a dark room, with your back to the window, you can also ask someone to set off a camera flash from behind you each time you hear thunder on the storm recording. The camera flash will simulate lightning. Imaginal exposure is difficult and takes much practice to use effectively. If you have problems becoming fearful while using imaginal exposure, don't give up. Keep practicing until it becomes easier, or try to use some of the other methods described in this section.

You may also find it useful to look at pictures or video footage of storms. You can probably find such materials on the Internet. Some examples of relevant Web sites include:

- http://www.stormchase.us

- http://www.weatherpictures.nl

- http://www.stormvideo.com/footage.html

- http://www.chaseday.com/lightning.htm

In addition to using imaginal exposure and exposures to pictures and videos, it is important to change your behaviors during actual storms. If being in certain rooms is frightening, stay in those rooms during the next storm. If looking out the window is difficult, look out the window during the next storm. Consider opening windows, standing outside with an umbrella, driving in the storm, being alone, and any other activities that might make your fears and phobias worse. With practice, these situations will become much easier. Use good judgment when planning practices. For example, some storms may not be safe for driving because of poor road conditions. If you are unsure whether your fear in a particular situation is realistic, ask someone who doesn't have an excessive fear of storms whether they would feel safe engaging in a particular practice.

Because storms are infrequent and unpredictable, you will have to take advantage of each storm as it occurs. Don't let a storm pass without trying some of the strategies discussed in the workbook. Make sure you have a plan for exposure before the storm occurs. Also, if you are in the habit of planning your activities around weather forecasts, you should stop watching weather reports until your fear of storms has improved.

Finally, simulated storms may provide opportunities for exposure. Some therapists have access to virtual reality (VR) computer software that will simulate the experience of sitting in a living room while there is a thunderstorm outside. You can check to see whether a therapist in your area offers VR treatments for storm phobias. One company (Virtually Better, Inc.) that produces such software for professionals has a list of VR therapists on their Web site (http://www.virtuallybetter.com).

There may be other simulated storms you can access. For example, Desert Passage (a shopping mall attached to the Aladdin Hotel in Las Vegas, Nevada) has a realistic simulated thunderstorm in the Merchant's Harbor area of the mall every 30 minutes. If you plan to check it out, be sure to confirm in advance that the simulated storm is still available (at the time of this writing, the hotel was being converted to a Planet Hollywood theme). Also, the planetarium at Vanderbilt Museum in Centerport, New York (on Long Island) has a show called *A Trip to the Planets,* which includes a simulated thunderstorm. Check with local planetariums and museums where you live to see if there is anything similar in your area.

Don't forget to review chapter 7 for a reminder of how exposure should be done. For example, it is important that practices are prolonged, frequent (e.g., at least several times per week), predictable, and planned. Don't fight the fear that arises—just let the feelings pass. With repeated practices, your fear of storms will decrease.

Despite being fairly common problems, choking and vomiting phobias have not been studied as thoroughly as some other phobias. Therefore, little is known about the prevalence and causes of these phobias. However, evidence from case studies suggests that choking phobias often begin with a traumatic near-choking experience. Furthermore, choking phobias can begin at any age and appear to be equally prevalent among men and women. Even less is known about the nature of vomiting phobias. However, one thing we do know is that fears of choking and vomiting are very treatable.

Overview of Treatment

The process of overcoming a fear of choking or vomiting involves three main components. The first step is *preparation*. Preparing to overcome your fear involves identifying the most important aspects of the problem, including the situations that trigger your fear, the variables that affect the intensity of your fear in these situations, the behaviors you use to protect yourself when feeling fearful, and the beliefs that contribute to your fear. The second component of treatment involves using the *cognitive strategies* discussed in chapter 6 to challenge your unrealistic, fearful predictions, and to replace them with more realistic thoughts. The third, and perhaps most important, component is *exposure* to the feared situation. Exposure involves confronting situations that frighten you, but it also involves stopping some of the unnecessary safety behaviors you currently use to protect yourself from possible danger, particularly when the true risk is minimal.

Identifying Triggers, Behaviors, and Thoughts

As discussed earlier, overcoming a fear of choking or vomiting will require using a variety of strategies. First, it is necessary to identify the specific triggers that affect your fear and anxiety. For each of these phobias, the presence of specific physical sensations (e.g., tightness in throat, nausea, gagging, suffocating sensations) can trigger anxiety. Similarly, eating specific foods may induce fear, particularly if those foods have caused choking or vomiting in the past. Foods that are particularly difficult for individuals with choking phobias include meat (especially with bones), certain dry foods, and some other solid foods. Most people with vomit phobias have numerous rules about which foods they can eat, although these rules vary from person to person. The presence of other "safe" people can decrease fears and phobias among individuals with choking and vomiting phobias. Make a list of all the sensations, foods, and other variables that trigger your fears and phobias of choking or vomiting.

In addition to identifying triggers, note the specific behaviors in which you engage because of your fear of choking or vomiting. For example, do you avoid eating alone? Do you chew your food excessively? Do you discard foods early to avoid possible spoilage that might lead you to be sick? Do you avoid being in places that make you tense? Do you avoid hospitals, places with young children, or other places where you might see someone vomit? Do you avoid going on amusement park rides, eating certain foods, drinking alcohol, getting a doctor's examination (e.g., because of the use of tongue depressors, thermometers), wearing certain clothing (e.g., ties, turtlenecks, scarves), reading in the car, or watching movies with scenes of vomiting or choking? Make a list of all the situations you avoid because of your fear. Be specific. Include subtle and obvious forms of avoidance (see chapter 3).

Finally, identify the fearful predictions you make involving choking and vomiting. Among people with choking phobias, the most common prediction is that they will choke to death. Individuals who fear vomiting often report a belief that the discomfort of vomiting will be unmanageable or that vomiting will lead to choking. In addition, they often fear the embarrassment of vomiting in a public place. People with vomiting and choking phobias often hold a variety of false beliefs about particular foods. They tend to believe that certain foods are more likely to lead to choking and vomiting when, in fact, there is no such relationship for most people.

Finally, people with choking and vomiting phobias typically misinterpret certain physical sensations as indicating that they are likely to choke or vomit. For example, a tightness or "lump" (also called *globus*) in the throat may be incorrectly interpreted as a sign that the throat is closing and that one cannot swallow. Or it may be seen as a signal that one is about to vomit. Actually, the sensation of globus in the throat is a normal feeling associated with many intense emotions (e.g., feeling afraid, being angry during a conflict, being on the verge of tears). The perceived inability to swallow that occurs in people with choking phobias happens because swallowing is under voluntary control, and people who fear choking tend to avoid swallowing because of their fear. In other words, the inability to swallow is fear-based, and not due to an actual closing of the throat.

In addition to the sensation of globus, other sensations (e.g., racing heart, unreality) might be interpreted as leading one to lose control, go crazy, faint, or do something embarrassing. What types of fearful predictions do you make involving choking and vomiting?

Changing Fearful Thoughts

Strategies for changing overestimations and catastrophic thoughts were discussed in detail in chapter 5. This process involves examining the evidence for your fearful predictions, and considering ways in which you could cope with the possibility of choking or vomiting (e.g., "Even if I actually threw up, it wouldn't be the end of the world—the discomfort would pass"), rather than focusing on how terrible the event would be if it were to occur (e.g., "It would be a disaster if I were to vomit"). We will not review these strategies here, so we recommend that you read chapter 5 again if necessary.

In addition to challenging overestimations and catastrophic thinking, it is important to learn whatever you can about choking or vomiting. For example, if you are fearful of choking, you should understand the reasons for choking. Specifically, choking occurs when food gets stuck in the windpipe (or trachea). This is most likely to happen when people eat quickly, move around too much as they eat, or inhale while swallowing. Although choking is rare, it can happen with almost any food or drink. Furthermore, it is no more likely to occur when you are wearing a tie or turtleneck shirt than when you are wearing loose-fitting clothes. Usually when we choke, it is relatively easy to dislodge the stuck food by coughing. First-aid courses provide instructions for dislodging stuck food in people for whom coughing doesn't work.

If you fear vomiting, learn whatever you can about it. Vomiting is a normal bodily response triggered when one eats something that the body interprets as undesirable or toxic. In some people, vomiting can be triggered by stress. However, if you have not vomited in a stressful situation so far, chances are that you are not one of those individuals. Interestingly, most people who fear vomiting rarely vomit. Vomiting can be triggered by a number of other situations, including having the flu, drinking too much alcohol, watching someone else vomit, and taking certain medications or vitamin supplements on an empty stomach. Vomiting is not at all dangerous unless it happens too often. For example, among those with bulimia who induce vomiting several times per day, vomiting can lead to damage to the throat and teeth and loss of important nutrients. However, under normal circumstances, vomiting is not at all dangerous.

We suggest that you make a list of questions that you have about vomiting or choking and set out to find answers at the library, a local bookstore, or on the Internet. Consider calling experts, including your family doctor, nurses, or first-aid specialists. The more you know about choking and vomiting, the less fearful you will feel.

Confronting Feared Situations Through Exposure

For most people with choking and vomiting phobias, exposure should include eating foods that lead to fear. People with choking phobias should begin to eat progressively more difficult foods. For example, if you fear eating meat or other solid foods, begin to eat more and more solid foods. If you fear swallowing pills, begin by swallowing small items (e.g., a cooked grain of rice) and work toward swallowing larger items. If you chew your food excessively, begin to swallow your food after a more "normal" amount of chewing. As one step becomes less frightening, move on to the next-most-difficult step on your hierarchy. It may take a long time to swallow at first, but it will get easier with practice.

In addition, it is important to begin to induce the sensations that make you fearful. If you avoid wearing tight clothing around your neck, work on wearing ties, scarves, and turtlenecks, and fastening your top shirt button. You can buy tongue depressors at your local drug store to induce a choking feeling or a gag reflex. If you fear vomiting, place a tongue depressor on the back of your tongue until you induce gagging (or you can use your toothbrush). If you are fearful of a nausea feeling, spin in a chair repeatedly to bring on this sensation. Chapter 7 describes methods of overcoming fears and phobias of sensations that are especially relevant to choking and vomiting phobias. Remember, the goal of these exercises is to experience feared sensations repeatedly until you learn that your feared consequences do not occur, or that you can cope.

If you are afraid of vomiting, an ideal exposure situation involves observing others vomit. Although it is difficult to set up such a situation in real life, there are numerous films that include vomiting scenes. These include dramas (e.g., *Leaving Las Vegas, Stand By Me*), horror films (e.g., *The Exorcist*), and comedies (e.g., *Monty Python's The Meaning of Life*). We recommend that you find the scenes with vomiting and watch them over and over until you learn that your feared consequences don't occur, or that they are manageable. If you have access to a novelty or joke store, buy some artificial vomit and practice looking at it. Or ask your helper or a friend to simulate vomiting (by making retching sounds). If watching another person pretend to vomit makes you fearful, practice doing this. Finally, consider making some of your own fake vomit. One recipe that was recommended to us by a therapist who treats vomit phobias calls for four parts oatmeal, two parts carrots and peas, and one part vinegar (blend well with a food processor or blender).

In most cases it is not necessary to actually induce vomiting to overcome your fear. However, if you find that the other strategies in this chapter are not enough to decrease your fear of vomiting, you may want to consider that option. The drug ipecac (derived from the ipecacuanha plant) is sometimes used to induce vomiting (e.g., following poisoning). However, there are risks associated with using this drug (or using other methods of inducing vomiting). The decision to induce vomiting should be made only after weighing the potential costs and benefits in consultation with your physician.

Water Phobias

Water phobias are relatively common. Almost 1 in 10 people has an extreme fear of water, and 3.4% of people report having a fear that is severe enough to be considered a water phobia (Curtis et al., 1998). Water phobias are about three times as common in women as in men (Bourdon et al., 1988). People who fear water usually avoid a variety of situations, including swimming, boating, crossing bridges over water, and standing near water (e.g., swimming pools).

Overview of Treatment

The process of overcoming a fear of water involves three main components. The first is *preparation*. Preparing to overcome your fear involves identifying the most important aspects of the problem, including the situations that trigger your fear, the variables that affect the intensity of your fear in these situations, the behaviors you use to protect yourself when feeling fearful, and the beliefs that contribute to your fear. The second component of treatment involves using the *cognitive strategies* discussed in chapter 6 to challenge your unrealistic, fearful predictions, and to replace them with more realistic thoughts. The third, and perhaps most important, component is *exposure* to the feared situation. Exposure involves confronting situations that frighten you, but it also involves stopping some of the unnecessary safety behaviors you currently use to protect yourself from possible danger, particularly when the true risk is minimal.

Identifying Triggers, Behaviors, and Thoughts

Before you can begin to overcome your fear of water, it is important to understand the triggers for your fear, your behavior when frightened, and the thoughts and beliefs are associated with your fear. Phobias are experienced differently by each individual, and the level of fear is greatly affected by numerous variables. Examples of factors that often affect levels of fear in people with water phobias include:

- Size of boat (e.g., cruise ship vs. canoe)

- Speed of boat

- Intensity of wind or other bad weather

- Size of waves

- Depth of water

- Type of water (e.g., ocean, lake, pool)

- Being alone vs. being accompanied by friends or family

- Location (e.g., near coast, right beside a pool, far from the water's edge)

- Time of day (day vs. night)

- Temperature of water

- Whether or not one is wearing a life jacket

- Presence of a life guard

- Ability to see the water (e.g., being on deck vs. in one's cabin on a cruise ship)

Are any of these relevant to your fear? What are some of the factors that make your fears and phobias stronger or weaker with respect to being around water?

In addition, it is necessary to note the specific behaviors in which you engage because of your fear of water. For example, do you avoid being near pools, lakes, and oceans? Do you avoid riding on boats? What about spending time in a hot tub or bath? Make a list of all the situations and activities you avoid that involve water. In addition, make a list of behaviors you use to protect yourself from "danger" when near water (e.g., staying near the edge, looking away from the water). These lists will help you identify the types of behaviors you will need to change to overcome your phobia.

Finally, identify the types of fearful predictions you make concerning water. Examples of negative beliefs often held by people who fear water include thoughts that the boat might tip; they might fall out of the boat or be pushed from it; they might become seasick, have no way to get help if there were an emergency (e.g., heart attack); and they might drown, be attacked by sharks or other aquatic animals, not be able to stay above water, not be able to get back to the shore in time, or not be able to swim. Many people also fear the sensations they experience while swimming. For example, a racing heart or breathlessness from the exercise might be interpreted as signs that one will not be able to stay above water and therefore will drown. Also, frightening sensations might be interpreted as signs of illness, or as leading to losing control, going crazy, fainting, or doing something embarrassing. What types of fearful predictions do you make regarding water? Identify as many fearful thoughts, predictions, and beliefs as you can.

Assessing and Improving Your Swimming Skills

It is possible you have good reason to be fearful of some situations involving water. For example, if you have never learned to swim, it is dangerous to spend extended periods of time in deep water, especially unsupervised. If your swimming skills are poor, we recommend that you take swimming lessons. Swimming classes are taught in a controlled setting (e.g., in a pool) with qualified instructors. If you explain to the instructor that you have a fear of water, he or she should be able to tailor the classes to your needs. If not, find an instructor who is more flexible in his or her teaching style. Swimming lessons will decrease your fear by providing exposure to situations involving water and giving you the skills you need to avoid accidents in deep water.

In addition, if you don't have the skills necessary to swim safely, we recommend that you take certain precautions. For example, don't swim in deep water alone. Also, wear a life jacket when boating. However, even if you cannot swim, there is no reason to completely avoid riding on boats, spending time in shallow water, and doing other similar activities.

Changing Fearful Thoughts

Strategies for changing overestimations and catastrophic thoughts were discussed in detail in chapter 5. Changing fearful thoughts involves examining the evidence for your fearful predictions and considering ways in which you could cope with being around water (e.g., "Even if I were to have a panic attack on a boat, the feeling would eventually pass"), rather than focusing on how terrible being near water would be (e.g., "I don't think I could manage if I had to be on a boat"). We will not review these strategies here, so we recommend that you read chapter 5 again if necessary.

In addition to challenging overestimations and catastrophic thinking, it is important to learn whatever you can about being in water. As discussed previously, swimming lessons are one way of doing this. Also, if you fear being attacked by sharks, you should make a point of learning where sharks are typically found. For example, sharks are not found in freshwater lakes. Nor are they typically found near heavily populated areas (e.g., beaches). Furthermore, popular beaches are continually monitored for dangerous swimming conditions (e.g., polluted water), and warnings are issued when appropriate. The risk of shark attacks is actually quite low. According to the Center for Shark Research at Florida's Mote Marine Laboratory, there are fewer than 100 shark attacks per year worldwide, and most of these are not fatal. In fact, a quote from George Burgess, the director of the University of Florida's International Shark Attack File, says it all: "Falling coconuts kill 150 people worldwide each year, 15 times the number of fatalities attributable to sharks" (http://unisci.com/stories/20022/0523024.htm).

If you notice yourself paying extra attention to news stories about people who drown, take note of all the individuals who don't drown. To make a realistic appraisal of aquatic dangers, pay attention to all relevant information (including all the people who aren't hurt while swimming and boating). We suggest that you make a list of questions that you have about boating, swimming, and other activities involving water, then set out to find answers to these questions by consulting books, the Internet, and experts (e.g., life guards, swimming instructors, boat owners). Don't just visit web sites on drowning. Also visit web sites about boating, swimming, water skiing, cruising, and other topics that are less likely to be focused on the danger of being near water. The more you know about being in the water, the less frightened you will be.

Confronting Feared Situations Through Exposure

Fortunately, it is easy to find situations involving water almost anywhere. Start by making a list of all the nearby places you can practice. These may include lakes, the ocean, ponds, and rivers. Also, make a list of friends and relatives who own pools. Are there health clubs in town with swimming pools? What about the YMCA? If your swimming skills are poor, find out where you can take swimming lessons. Even if you choose not to take lessons at the beginning, you should still find out where you can practice being in the water. Most pools and beaches have large areas of shallow water. Finding a place to swim will require some research, but it shouldn't be too difficult.

If boating frightens you, find out where you could practice boating. Do you have any friends or relatives who own boats? If not, are there marinas near your home that rent paddleboats, fishing boats, or canoes? Make a list of places where you could practice being on boats. If there is nowhere near your home to practice taking a boat, plan a vacation to a place near water, or take a cruise. If you practice taking boat rides daily for a week or two, you will notice a decrease in your fear.

Because you have avoided water for some time, you may be unaware of all the places where you can swim and use boats. If you can't think of places to practice, ask other people for suggestions. Also, your telephone directory or the travel section of your newspaper are great places to start.

Homework

✎ Complete the steps discussed in this chapter to overcome your phobia.

✎ Review earlier chapters as necessary—especially chapters 3, 5, and 7. Use the forms and tools presented in those earlier chapters to help you use the strategies discussed in this chapter.

Recommended Reading

Animal Phobia

Antony, M. M., & McCabe, R. E. (2005). *Overcoming animal and insect phobias: How to conquer fear of dogs, snakes, rodents, bees, spiders, and more.* Oakland, CA: New Harbinger.

Blood and Needle Phobia

Antony, M. M., & Watling, M. (2006). *Overcoming medical phobias: How to conquer fear of blood, needles, doctors, and dentists.* Oakland, CA: New Harbinger.

Driving Phobia

Joseph, J. (2003). *110 car and driving emergencies and how to survive them: The complete guide to staying safe on the road.* Guilford, CT: Lyons.

Triffitt, J. (2003). *Back in the driver's seat: Understanding, challenging and managing the fear of driving.* Tasmania, Australia: Dr. Jacqui Triffitt. Copies of this book may be ordered from http://www.backinthe driversseat.com.au.

Flying Phobia

Akers-Douglas, A., & Georgiou, G. (1996). *Flying? No fear! A handbook for apprehensive fliers.* West Sussex, UK: Summersdale.

Brown, D. (1996). *Flying without fear.* Oakland, CA: New Harbinger Publications.

Cronin, J. (1998). *Your flight questions answered by a jetliner pilot.* Vergennes, VT: Plymouth.

Evans, J. (1997). *All you ever wanted to know about flying: The passenger's guide to how airliners fly.* Osceola, WI: Motorbooks International.

Hartman, C., & Huffaker, J.S. (1995). *The fearless flyer: How to fly in comfort and without trepidation.* Portland, OR: Eighth Mountain.

Seaman, D. (1998). *The fearless flier's handbook: Learning to beat the fear of flying with the experts from the Qantas Clinic.* Berkeley, CA: Ten Speed.

Smith, P. (2004). *Ask the pilot: Everything you need to know about air travel.* New York: Riverhead.

Height Phobia

Antony, M. M., & Rowa, K. (2007). *Overcoming fear of heights.* Oakland, CA: New Harbinger.

References

American Psychiatric Association. (2000). *Diagnostic and statistical manual of mental disorders* (4th ed., Text revision). Washington, DC: American Psychiatric Association.

Antony, M. M., & Barlow, D. H. (2002). Specific phobia. In D. H. Barlow (Ed.), *Anxiety and its disorders: The nature and treatment of anxiety and panic* (2nd ed., pp. 380–417). New York: Guilford.

Antony, M. M., McCabe, R. E., Leeuw, I., Sano, N., & Swinson, R. P. (2001). Effect of exposure and coping style on in vivo exposure for specific phobia of spiders. *Behaviour Research and Therapy, 39,* 1137–1150.

Baker, B. L., Cohen, D. C., & Saunders, J. T. (1973). Self-directed desensitization for acrophobia. *Behaviour Research and Therapy, 11,* 79–89.

Beckham, J. C., Vrana, S. R., May, J. G., Gustafson, D. J., & Smith, G. R. (1990). Emotional processing and fear measurement synchrony as indicators of treatment outcome in fear of flying. *Journal of Behavior Therapy and Experimental Psychiatry, 21,* 153–162.

Bourdon, K. H., Boyd, J. H., Rae, D. S., Burns, B. J., Thompson, J. W., & Locke, B. Z. (1988). Gender differences in phobias: Results of the ECA community study. *Journal of Anxiety Disorders, 2,* 227–241.

Bourque, P., & Ladouceur, R. (1980). An investigation of various performance-based treatments with acrophobics. *Behaviour Research and Therapy, 18,* 161–170.

Craske, M. G., Mohlman, J., Yi, J., Glover, D., & Valeri, S. (1995). Treatment of claustrophobias and snake/spider phobias: Fear of arousal and fear of context. *Behaviour Research and Therapy, 33,* 197–203.

Curtis, G. C., Magee, W. J., Eaton, W. W., Wittchen, H.-U., & Kessler, R. C. (1998). Specific fears and phobias: Epidemiology and classification. *British Journal of Psychiatry, 173,* 212–217.

Foa, E. B., Blau, J. S., Prout, M., & Latimer, P. (1977). Is horror a necessary component of flooding (implosion)? *Behaviour Research and Therapy, 15,* 397–402.

Fredrikson, M., Annas, P., Fischer, H., & Wik, G. (1996). Gender and age differences in the prevalence of specific fears and phobias. *Behaviour Research and Therapy, 26,* 241–244.

Fyer, A. J., Mannuzza, S., Gallops, M. S., Martin, L. Y., Aaronson, C., Gorman, J. G., et al. (1990). Familial transmission of simple phobias and fears. *Archives of General Psychiatry, 47,* 252–256.

Gauthier, J., & Marshall, W. L. (1977). The determination of optimal exposure to phobic stimuli in flooding therapy. *Behaviour Research and Therapy, 15,* 403–410.

Gitin, N. M., Herbert, J. D., & Schmidt, C. (1996, November). *One-session in vivo exposure for odontophobia.* Paper presented at the meeting of the Association for Advancement of Behavior Therapy, New York, NY.

Greenberg, D. B., Stern, T. A., & Weilburg, J. B. (1988). The fear of choking: Three successfully treated cases. *Psychosomatics, 29,* 126–129.

Hellström, K., & Öst, L.-G. (1995). One-session therapist directed exposure vs. two forms of manual directed self-exposure in the treatment of spider phobia. *Behaviour Research and Therapy, 33,* 959–965.

Hepner, A., & Cauthen, N. R. (1975). Effect of subject control and graduated exposure on snake phobias. *Journal of Consulting and Clinical Psychology, 43,* 297–304.

Hettema, J. M., M. C. Neale, and K. S. Kendler. 2001. A review and meta-analysis of the genetic epidemiology of anxiety disorders. *American Journal of Psychiatry 158,* 1568–1578.

Houlihan, D., Schwartz, C., Miltenberger, R., Heuton, D. (1993). The rapid treatment of a young man's balloon (noise) phobia using in vivo flooding. *Journal of Behavior Therapy and Experimental Psychiatry, 24,* 233–240.

Howard, W. A., Murphy, S. M., & Clarke, J. C. (1983). The nature and treatment of fear of flying: A controlled investigation. *Behavior Therapy, 14,* 557–567.

Kendler, K. S., Karkowski, L. M., & Prescott, C. A. (1999). Fear and phobias: Reliability and heritability. *Psychological Medicine, 29,* 539–553.

Kessler, R. C., Berglund, P., Demler, O., Jin, R., Merikangas, K. R., & Walters, E. E. (2005). Lifetime prevalence and age-of-onset distributions of DSM-IV disorders in the National Comorbidity Survey Replication. *Archives of General Psychiatry, 62,* 593–602.

Kleinknecht, R. A., & Lenz, J. (1989). Blood/injury fear, fainting, and avoidance of medically related situations: A family correspondence study. *Behaviour Research and Therapy, 27,* 537–547.

Kozak, M. J., & Miller, G. A. (1985). The psychophysiological process of therapy in a case of injury-scene-elicited fainting. *Journal of Behavior Therapy and Experimental Psychiatry, 16,* 139–145.

Kozak, M. J., & Montgomery, G. K. (1981). Multimodal behavioral treatment of recurrent injury-scene elicited fainting (vasodepressor syncope). *Behavioural Psychotherapy, 9,* 316–321.

Lang, A. J., & Craske, M. G. (2000). Manipulations of exposure based therapy to reduce return of fear: A replication. *Behaviour Research and Therapy, 38,* 1–12.

Menzies, R. G., & Clarke, J. C. (1993). A comparison of in vivo and vicarious exposure in the treatment of childhood water phobia. *Behaviour Research and Therapy, 31,* 9–15.

Moore, R., and Brødsgaard, I. (1994). Group therapy compared with individual desensitization for dental anxiety. *Community Dentistry and Oral Epidemiology, 22,* 258–262.

Muris, P., Mayer, B., & Merckelbach, H. (1998). Trait anxiety as a predictor of behaviour therapy outcome in spider phobia. *Behavioural and Cognitive Psychotherapy, 26,* 87–91.

Mystkowski, J., Craske, M. G., & Echiverri, E. (2002) Treatment context and return of fear in spider phobia. *Behavior Therapy, 33,* 399–416.

Mystkowski, J., Echiverri, A., Labus, J., & Craske, M. G. (in press). Mental reinstatement of context and return of fear in spider phobia. *Behavior Therapy.*

Öst, L.-G. (1978). Behavioral treatment of thunder and lightning phobias. *Behaviour Research and Therapy, 16,* 197–207.

Öst, L.-G. (1987). Age of onset of different phobias. *Journal of Abnormal Psychology, 96,* 223–229.

Öst, L.-G. (1989). One-session treatment for specific phobias. *Behaviour Research and Therapy, 27,* 1–7.

Öst, L.-G. (1992). Blood and injection phobia: Background and cognitive, physiological, and behavioral variables. *Journal of Abnormal Psychology, 101,* 68–74.

Öst, L.-G. (1996). Long term effects of behavior therapy for specific phobia. In M. R. Mavissakalian and R. F. Prien (Eds.), *Long-term treatments of the anxiety disorders* (pp. 121–170). Washington, DC: American Psychiatric Press.

Öst, L.-G., Brandberg, M., & Alm, T. (1997). One versus five sessions of exposure in the treatment of flying phobia. *Behaviour Research and Therapy, 35,* 987–996.

Öst, L.-G., Fellenius, J., & Sterner, U. (1991). Applied tension, exposure *in vivo,* and tension-only in the treatment of blood phobia. *Behaviour Research and Therapy, 29,* 561–574.

Öst, L.-G., Ferebee, I., & Furmark, T. (1997). One-session group therapy of spider phobia: Direct versus indirect treatments. *Behaviour Research and Therapy, 35,* 721–732.

Öst, L.-G., Johansson, J., & Jerremalm, A. (1982). Individual response patterns and the effects of different behavioral methods in the treatment of claustrophobia. *Behaviour Research and Therapy, 20,* 445–460.

Öst, L.-G., Salkovskis, P. M., & Hellström, K. (1991). One-session therapist directed exposure vs. self-exposure in the treatment of spider phobia. *Behavior Therapy, 22,* 407–422.

Öst, L.-G., & Sterner, U. (1987). Applied tension: A specific behavioral method for treatment of blood phobia. *Behaviour Research and Therapy, 25,* 25–29.

Page, A. C., and N. G. Martin. 1998. Testing a genetic structure of blood-injury-injection fears. *American Journal of Medical Genetics, 81,* 377–384.

Rachman, S. (1976). The passing of the two-stage theory of fear and avoidance: Fresh possibilities. *Behaviour Research and Therapy, 14,* 125–131.

Rachman, S. (1977). The conditioning theory of fear-acquisition: A critical examination. *Behaviour Research and Therapy, 15,* 375–387.

Rowe, M. K., & Craske, M. G. (1998). Effects of an expanding-spaced versus massed exposure schedule. *Behaviour Research and Therapy, 36,* 701–717.

Seligman, M. E. P. (1971). Phobias and preparedness. *Behavior Therapy, 2,* 307–320.

Tsao, J. C. I., & Craske, M. G. (2001). Timing of treatment and return of fear: Effects of massed, uniform and expanding spaced exposure schedules. *Behavior Therapy, 31,* 479–497.

About the Authors

Martin M. Antony, PhD, is a professor in the department of psychology at Ryerson University in Toronto, and the director of research at the Anxiety Treatment and Research Centre at St. Joseph's Healthcare in Hamilton, Ontario. He received his doctorate in clinical psychology from the University at Albany, State University of New York, and completed his predoctoral internship training at the University of Mississippi Medical Center in Jackson. Antony has written 20 books and more than 100 articles and book chapters in the areas of cognitive behavior therapy, obsessive-compulsive disorder, panic disorder, social phobia, and specific phobia. Antony has received career awards from the Society of Clinical Psychology (American Psychological Association), the Canadian Psychological Association, and the Anxiety Disorders Association of America, and is a Fellow of the American and Canadian Psychological Associations. He has also served on the boards of directors for the Society of Clinical Psychology and the Association for Behavioral and Cognitive Therapies, and as the program chair for past conventions of the Association for Advancement of Behavior Therapy and the Anxiety Disorders Association of America. Antony is actively involved in clinical research in the area of anxiety disorders, he teaches, and he maintains a clinical practice. He is also a diplomate in clinical psychology of the American Board of Professional Psychology.

Michelle G. Craske received her PhD from the University of British Columbia in 1985 and has authored more than 160 articles and chapters in the area of anxiety disorders. She has written books on the topics of the etiology and treatment of anxiety disorders, gender differences in anxiety, and translation from the basic science of fear learning to the clinical application of understanding and treating phobias, and has written several self-help books. In addition, she has been the recipient of continuous NIMH funding since 1991 for research projects pertaining to risk factors for anxiety disorders and depression among children and adolescents, the cognitive and physiological aspects of anxiety and panic attacks, and the development and dissemination of treatments for anxiety and related disorders. She is an associate editor for the *Journal of Abnormal Psychology* and for *Behaviour*

Research and Therapy and is a Scientific Board Member for the Anxiety Disorders Association of America. She was a member of the *DSM–IV* Anxiety Disorders Work Group Subcommittee to revise the diagnostic criteria for panic disorder and specific phobia. Craske has given invited keynote addresses at many international conferences and is frequently invited to present training workshops on the most recent advances in the cognitive behavioral treatment for anxiety disorders. She is currently a professor in the department of psychology and in the department of psychiatry and biobehavioral sciences, at the University of California in Los Angeles (UCLA) and is the director of the UCLA Anxiety Disorders Behavioral Research Program.

David H. Barlow received his PhD from the University of Vermont in 1969 and has authored more than 500 articles and chapters, and close to 50 books and clinical workbooks, mostly in the area of emotional disorders and clinical research methodology. The book and workbooks have been translated into more than 20 languages, including Arabic, Mandarin, and Russian.

He was formerly a professor of psychiatry at the University of Mississippi Medical Center and a professor of psychiatry and psychology at Brown University and founded clinical psychology internships in both settings. He was also a Distinguished Professor in the department of psychology at the University at Albany, State University of New York. Currently, he is a professor of psychology, a research professor of psychiatry, and the director of the Center for Anxiety and Related Disorders at Boston University.

Barlow is the recipient of the 2000 American Psychological Association (APA) Distinguished Scientific Award for the Applications of Psychology; First Annual Science Dissemination Award from the Society for a Science of Clinical Psychology of the APA; and the 2000 Distinguished Scientific Contribution Award from the Society of Clinical Psychology of the APA. He also received an award in appreciation for outstanding achievements from the General Hospital of the Chinese People's Liberation Army, Beijing, China, with an appointment as Honorary Visiting Professor of Clinical Psychology. During the 1997/1998 academic year, he was the Fritz Redlich Fellow at the Center for Advanced Study in Behavioral Sciences, in Palo Alto, California.

Other awards include Career Contribution Awards from the Massachusetts, California, and Connecticut Psychological Associations; the 2004 C. Charles

Burlingame Award from the Institute of Living in Hartford, Connecticut; the first Graduate Alumni Scholar Award from the Graduate College, University of Vermont; the Masters and Johnson Award, from the Society for Sex Therapy and Research; the G. Stanley Hall Lectureship, American Psychological Association; a certificate of appreciation for contributions to women in clinical psychology from Section IV of Division 12 of the APA, the Clinical Psychology of Women; and a MERIT award from the National Institute of Mental Health for long-term contributions to the clinical research effort. He is a past president of the Society of Clinical Psychology of the American Psychological Association and the Association for the Advancement of Behavior Therapy, a past editor of the journals *Behavior Therapy, Journal of Applied Behavior Analysis,* and *Clinical Psychology: Science and Practice,* and the current editor-in-chief of the Treatments *ThatWork*™ series for Oxford University Press.

He was the chair of the American Psychological Association Task Force of Psychological Intervention Guidelines, was a member of the *DSM–IV* Task Force of the American Psychiatric Association, and was a co-chair of the work group for revising the anxiety-disorder categories. He is also a diplomate in clinical psychology of the American Board of Professional Psychology and maintains a private practice.